Politics, Power, & *Playboy*

Politics, Power, & Playboy is part of the Virginia Tech Student Publications series. This series contains book-length works authored and edited by Virginia Tech undergraduate and graduate students and published in collaboration with VT Publishing. Often these books are the culmination of class projects for advanced or capstone courses. The series provides the opportunity for students to write, edit, and ultimately publish their own books for the world to learn from and enjoy.

Politics, Power, & *Playboy*

The American Mindset of the 1960s

છે

A Class Project by the Students in
the Department of History at Virginia Tech

Edited by
Dr. Marian Mollin

VIRGINIA TECH™

Virginia Tech Department of History
in Association with VT Publishing
Blacksburg, VA

Copyright © 2019 Virginia Tech
Individual chapters copyright © 2019 respective authors

First published 2019 by the Virginia Tech Department of History in association with VT Publishing.

Virginia Tech Department of History
431 Major Williams Hall
220 Stanger Street
Blacksburg, VA 24061

VT Publishing
University Libraries at Virginia Tech
560 Drillfield Dr.
Blacksburg, VA 24061

The collection and its individual chapters are covered by the following Creative Commons License:

Attribution-NonCommercial-NoDerivatives 4.0 International (CC BY-NC-ND 4.0)

You are free to:

Share — Copy and redistribute the material in any medium or format. The licensor cannot revoke these freedoms as long as you follow the license terms.

Under the following terms:

Attribution — You must give appropriate credit, provide a link to the license, and indicate if changes were made. You may do so in any reasonable manner, but not in any way that suggests the licensor endorses you or your use.

NonCommercial — You may not use the material for commercial purposes.

NoDerivatives — If you remix, transform, or build upon the material, you may not distribute the modified material.

No additional restrictions — You may not apply legal terms or technological measures that legally restrict others from doing anything the license permits.

The above is a summary of the full license, which is available at the following URL:
https://creativecommons.org/licenses/by-nc-nd/4.0/

ISBN: 978-1-949373-10-3 (paperback)
ISBN: 978-1-949373-11-0 (PDF)
ISBN: 978-1-949373-12-7 (epub)

DOI: https://doi.org/10.21061/politics-power-playboy

Every effort has been made to contact and acknowledge copyright owners, but the authors would be pleased to have any errors or omissions brought to their attention, so that corrections may be published in future editions.

Book cover design by Seth Hendrickson and Gia Theocharidis. See cover image credits on p. 161.

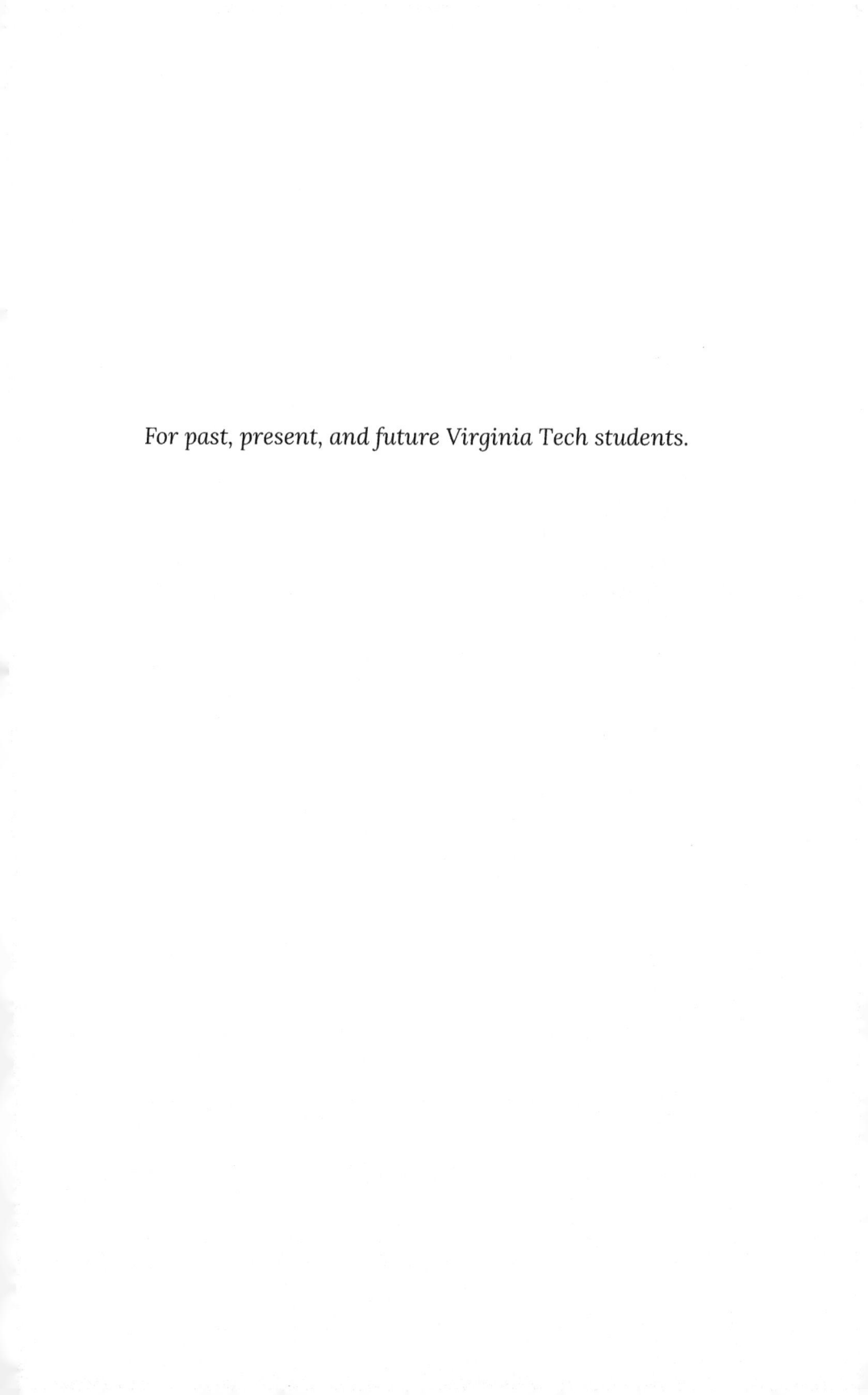

For past, present, and future Virginia Tech students.

The thing the sixties did was to show us the possibilities and the responsibility that we all had. It wasn't the answer. It just gave us a glimpse of the possibility.

— John Lennon, interview with David Sholin of RKO radio, December 1980

Contents

	Introduction	1
1.	The Battle for Political Predominance: The Development of the California Conservative and Liberal Identity Brett Kershaw	5
2.	John F. Kennedy: A Man of the People Abigail Simko	21
3.	Red on the Horizon: The Cuban Missile Crisis and the 1963 Limited Test Ban Treaty Seth Hendrickson	37
4.	Atlanta's Model Cities Program: A Boondoggle, Farce, and Ultimate Failure Brianna Sclafani	55
5.	Comparing Rivals: Antiwar Protests at the University of Virginia and Virginia Tech Frank Powell	73
6.	SNCC Identity: From Interracial Nonviolence to Black Power Kayla Mizelle	87
7.	The Color of Culture: The Black Power Movement and American Popular Culture Gia Theocharidis	105
8.	Black Is Beautiful: Mirroring the Media Claire Ko	121
9.	*Cosmopolitan* and *Playboy*: Complicated Beauty Ideals and 1960s Feminism Kaya McGee	139
	Notes on Contributors	155

| Acknowledgments | 159 |
| Cover Image Credits | 161 |

Introduction

This collection of essays grew out of a class project for our Spring 2019 Capstone History Research Seminar, "America in the 1960s," at Virginia Tech. Taken together, the chapters emphasize what became an important and reoccurring theme in our class discussions: the contestation of power in multiple realms. Students selected a topic of their choice and developed their ideas into a semester-long project. Throughout the writing process the themes of politics, power, and *Playboy* came to light, which we used as a thematic guide. Working together as a class, we crafted a title, identified the volume's organizing themes, and decided on the order of the chapters. Several of our classmates also designed the cover and chose a quote for the epigraph. While our professor, Dr. Marian Mollin, served as "head coach" and developmental editor, this book is the product of an intentionally collective student-centered effort that drew on all of our interests and skills.

This volume's initial four chapters focus on American **politics** over the course of the 1960s. Although this section only provides a glimpse of American society during the 1960s, these four chapters highlight the transformative impact this decade had on American political life. The first two chapters focus on electoral politics. Chapter one examines the unique relationship between Californian liberalism and conservatism. Their development in California's gubernatorial elections produced rigid ideological contrasts between the Democratic and Republican parties that reflected the increasingly polarized rhetoric of national politics. Chapter two analyzes public support for President John F. Kennedy during his run for office, during his time in the presidency, and in the aftermath that followed his assassination in 1963. Although Kennedy may have been mythologized after his death, public support for him was consistently solid throughout the period this chapter studies. This ongoing support helps explain the impact of his assassination on Americans throughout the rest of the decade by creating a long-standing legacy that nevertheless had deep roots.

If the first two chapters highlight political attitudes and beliefs, the next two emphasize the making and implementation of policy. Chapter three moves us into the realm of foreign policy, in particular how the United States and the Soviet Union overcame long-standing differences and enacted a nuclear test ban treaty following the 1962 Cuban Missile Crisis. The combination of driven and cooperative leadership between Kennedy and Khrushchev, as well as advances in technology and testing, allowed a shift in negotiations between the two super powers that marked a significant change in American foreign policy. Chapter four returns to the arena of domestic policy by examining the failure of Atlanta's Model Cities Program. Here the author analyzes how the program's discriminatory practices perpetuated racial and economic segregation and influenced how black and white Americans viewed the antipoverty program. Moreover, this research emphasizes the link between politics and power by highlighting how black and white political actors battled for authority over the Model Cities Program.

The three chapters that compose this volume's second section, while quite different from each other in focus, together describe a similar intensity in struggles for *power* in 1960s America. As these chapters make clear, power came wrapped in many packages. It manifested itself as local resistance, as large-scale student protest, and as the celebration of racial pride. During the 1960s, different social, cultural, and political factions vied for power. This section examines how groups such as African Americans and white college students struggled for ways to claim their voices and make their choices as free citizens. The Black Power and Student Protest movements thus encapsulated much of the turmoil of the decade. The first power struggle this section examines is the student antiwar movement. While stories from Northern and elite universities drive the historical narrative of the resistance to the Vietnam War, chapter five analyzes and compares protests at two southern colleges, the University of Virginia and Virginia Tech, in order to broaden the scope of our understanding of this movement. This chapter also provides further research to support the idea that the movement was not one massive uniform entity, but a conglomeration of movements shaped by the cultures of specific colleges as much as by geographic location.

The next two chapters focus on complicated relationships between race and power. Chapter six discusses the Student Nonviolent Coordinating Committee (SNCC) and its rhetorical shift from interracial nonviolence to black power. This chapter examines three different time periods of the organization and pinpoints the moments in which SNCC's ideas about identity evolved. Chapter seven examines the influence of the Black Power struggle on American popular culture: with a specific focus on pop music and holiday celebrations. This chapter argues that while the movement worked to make a popular culture that had been geared towards a white audience more inclusive for black Americans, it also led to the formation of a separate, new African American cultural identity.

The final section of the book discusses how popular media reflected the shift in ideas about women's sexuality and beauty standards over the course of the 1960s. The transformation of these ideals came in response to large-scale movements such as the sexual revolution and Black Power. Together, these last two chapters demonstrate how radical ideas within these movements played an important role in shaping how magazines and newspapers – from **Playboy** to *Cosmpolitan* to *Ebony* – portrayed sexuality and beauty to national audiences. The impact of these social movements on popular beauty standards highlights the important link between the personal and political for both black and white women.

Chapter eight analyzes the role that Black Power symbols, such as afros and darker skin, played in shaping what the images portrayed in advertisements in popular black magazines and newspapers. The Black is Beautiful movement, a sub-movement of Black Power, influenced the slow integration of diverse models that did not conform to the white ideal. The movement and its activists transformed how the general public perceived beauty by promoting and celebrating distinctly black aesthetic ideals. Chapter nine analyzes the relationship between the combined feminist and sexual revolutions to cover images on two popular and highly sexualized magazines, *Cosmopolitan* and *Playboy*. These movements of liberation allowed women to redefine their perceptions of beauty and sexuality independently from men. Although their freedom expanded within these social changes, the magazine media outlets did not reflect the full evolution of female self-expression.

The sixties was truly an era of reform and revolution. While each of these chapters are vastly different from one another, what they provide as a collective whole is a way to examine the scope of what happened in the 1960s. Politics, power, and *Playboy* were not as different as one may believe.

1. The Battle for Political Predominance: The Development of the California Conservative and Liberal Identity

BRETT KERSHAW

Despite liberalism's national ascendancy in the early 1960s, California was alternatively a place where liberal and conservative ideals both garnered popular public support. Beginning in 1958, California's incumbent governor, Edmund "Pat" Brown, had crafted a unique governing philosophy around an adaptive set of political principles that coalesced into a new liberal platform. Nonetheless, as the decade continued, a vocal populous in the state's wealthy southern suburbs developed the foundations of the American conservative movement and positioned its support around the 1960 Republican presidential nominee, Richard Nixon, and former Hollywood actor Ronald Reagan.[1] In this setting, these individuals became the initial public figures to exemplify the beliefs of California liberalism and conservatism.

As the decade continued, these beliefs became central to California gubernatorial politics. Brown's electoral victory signified that for the first time since World War II, a Democrat could attract an electoral majority in the state.[2] However for Brown, the "Democrat" label next to his name failed to indicate the importance of his adoption of what were not traditionally combined liberal principles. At the same time, throughout the tenure of his governorship, Brown's ideological values were continually challenged by an anti-statist conservative movement embraced by the state's suburban voters. Over time, these ideological factions – liberal and conservative – clashed as they crusaded for the seat of governor and dedicated political campaigns that strategically outlined their principles and denounced those of the other.

Authors have offered a wide range of perspectives and arguments on the importance of California liberalism and conservatism. Scholars studying the development of California liberalism attribute its success in the Brown administration to California's increasingly diverse population and growing calls for economic and racial justice. However, authors studying the rise of California conservatism indicate the movement succeeded in obtaining popular support during Reagan's gubernatorial administration by supporting a restoration of limited governance, social order, and moral decency. These scholarly studies pursue the common structure of describing the development of these ideological factions in isolation, and in the process fail to compare their relationships and the political interactions that occurred over the course of the 1960s. The development of interaction between these countering ideologies is rarely addressed, but provides valuable insight on the relationship between liberalism and conservatism during this time.[3]

This chapter aims to explore the relationship between 1960s California liberalism and conservatism by examining the gubernatorial races of 1962 and 1966. By addressing the attitudes and beliefs that defined each ideology's principles, it becomes possible to understand how conservative and liberal beliefs influenced each other during this critical period in American politics. What were the core components of conservative and liberal beliefs, ideals, and policy recommendations? How did Brown, Nixon, and Reagan formulate their political platform and express their beliefs to the general public? And in what ways did these beliefs influence each other? Between 1958 and 1966, these conflicting worldviews fought for political and ideological dominance, shaping the mainstream of the United States' political culture in ways that still reverberate today. Asking and answering these questions thus provides an understanding of the past, but also of how liberal and conservative thought manifests itself today.

For each of these ideologies, their representation of the "preferred" American society indicated their acceptance of core political notions. Their transformation from visionary rhetoric into political policy turned conservative and liberal beliefs into rigid party platforms. In the process, Republican and Democratic critiques of their opponents' political platforms led to the articulation of distinctively conservative and liberal visions of California, and of America. In other words, neither political perspective developed solely on its own. As this chapter demonstrates, their interactions with each other were critical to modern liberal and conservative beliefs.

Brown's victory in the Golden State gave hope to California liberals. His 1958 campaign highlighted an array of prominent liberal ideals that called for increased spending for state programs and the expansion of rights to politically unprotected groups.[4] In 1958, this revision to the liberal platform was unique to California. The influence of New Deal fiscal policies increased the importance of regulating markets and expanding social programs, but did little to directly combat racial discrimination.[5] Liberals believed that California's growing population resulted from years of state-led economic development.[6] With minority groups becoming a prominent portion of this growing population, their importance to the Democratic Party became vital. Blending a nuanced vision of racial equality with the historic liberal principle of economic equality led to the creation of a new ideology. Under Brown, the culmination of these ideas garnered public support as he won the governorship in 1958.

Brown's vision of California society, however, was not uniformly accepted. As liberal policy grew in popular support, a growing concern with American liberalism's electoral dominance linked social conservatives to free-market oriented businessmen and libertarians.[7] Unlike earlier incarnations, 1960s California conservatism united ideological factions that formerly had been disconnected. Fueled by their discontent over liberalism, a hawkish anti-communist attitude, and their commitment to limited state governance, families, businessmen, and religious organizations embraced California conservatism as the rational approach to politics.[8] By 1962, the California Republican Party revitalized a variety of conservative principles that took aim at combating liberalism's stronghold under the Brown administration.

After 1958, the politics of California's gubernatorial office became increasingly partisan. With new popular, competing political ideologies, Democratic and Republican leaders saw the 1962 gubernatorial race as a measure of their influence. Conservatives considered Richard Nixon a tenured politician, with experience as vice president under Dwight E. Eisenhower, who could spearhead California's conservative movement. Nixon's historic cooperation with moderate factions in the Republican Party challenged the hard-line conservative stance embraced by vocal groups, such as the John Birch Society. Moderate conservative leaders, however, sought to separate their principles from radical right wing organizations.[9] By 1962, a reinvigorated conservative movement, led by the moderates and with Nixon at the helm, aimed to usurp Brown's governorship and introduce "common-sense" conservatism to the state.

For both candidates, the governor's office was key to their success as a politician, but their victories would also indicate an ideological triumph for each of their visions for American society. During the 1962 race, the Nixon campaign relied on a new conservative coalition being crafted in the state's suburbs. His campaign embraced popular conservative sentiments, such as calls for decreasing government programs and lowering taxes.[10] Brown's progressive policy aspirations, however, attracted support from other groups of Californians. Running on a platform of continuing the liberal status quo, Brown utilized his past political successes and defeated Richard Nixon handily in the 1962 race.[11] At the end of Brown's first term, Californians had responded kindly to the progressive programs undertaken during his administration. This victory appeared to indicate liberalism's supremacy in California politics.

By 1966, Brown had led the liberal status quo for eight years as governor, but his third campaign for reelection would be tested by a hardened conservative movement. After 1962, California conservatives were defeated. And after Goldwater's defeat in the 1964 Presidential election, California conservatism's future seemed even more unclear.[12] By 1965, however, conservatives rejoiced as Ronald Reagan accepted the Republican Party nomination for governor. Reagan believed that liberalism had tainted the state's moral decency. Highlighting tumultuous events at the University of California, Berkeley, and other state universities, Reagan attracted large support throughout the state.[13] In contrast to his 1962 campaign, in 1966, Brown failed to counter Reagan's vigorous support among Californians.[14] Since 1958, Brown had led the state's liberal platform while embracing the progressive steps he made while in office, but he could not defeat Reagan's rebranded conservative movement in 1966. After eight years, liberal and conservative principles faced public critique and support, and after two gubernatorial elections, the California conservative movement took the office of governor and the symbolic control of the state's politics.

In general terms, a political vision is defined by a set of ideological principles and governing policy aspirations. For California, the creation of liberal and conservative ideologies produced a conflicting set of outlines for societal structures and relationships. These conflicting visions were often more idealistic than pragmatic. However, based on their contrasting ideals, Democrats and Republicans offered different perspectives on the role of government, the power of the government, and the role of the populace. Within the 1962 and 1966 gubernatorial races, these visions developed and, despite their differences, at times mirrored each other.

California's liberal vision was founded upon the idea of progressive state governance. This concept was first characterized in Governor Brown's first inaugural address. Understanding that his election signified the victory of liberal beliefs, Brown proclaimed, "Offered reaction by the radical right, the voters emphatically declined. Offered government by retreat, the people preferred progress. Clearly then, our duty is to bring to California the forward force of responsible liberalism."[15] To Brown, an egalitarian Californian society could only be achieved under the progress afforded in "responsible liberalism." His progressive vision aimed to uproot the practices of racial discrimination and economic stagnation. For Brown, these societal ills would not be addressed under conservative governance. His vision assumed that "responsible liberalism" could eradicate social inequity through governmental aid and involvement. He outlined this belief broadly as "a genuine concern and deep respect for all the people."[16] Brown believed that Californians deserved "the right to demand protection from economic abuse and selfish threats to his security."[17] In Brown's first inaugural, his speech outlined a liberal agenda that would address the inequitable conditions of California society through progressive governance. This vision – an ideal California society rid of racial inequality and economic inequality – framed the liberal ideals embraced by Brown's administration.

As state governance shifted toward the left, conservatives challenged the liberal status quo by producing a contrasting set of values for California society. In 1960, the presidential election of John F. Kennedy further signified liberalism's apparent triumph. Nonetheless, California's conservative Republicans utilized opposition to Brown's liberal agenda to articulate a distinct and opposing political vision. Basing their vision off a free-market approach to fiscal procedures and a governing structure that protected freedoms and societal equities through selected and limited state interference, the conservative movement clashed with the liberal approach to progressive governance.[18] At first, these values resonated mostly in the state's wealthy southern suburb of Orange County. However, after four years of liberal

Democratic governance, this newly formulated conservative vision would be publicly supported by the Republican Party under Richard Nixon in the 1962 gubernatorial race.[19]

By the 1962 gubernatorial race, conservative values had manifested in opposition to Brown's liberal agenda. Nonetheless, Governor Brown met the conservative tide directly by saying, "Nixon thinks everything California is doing is wrong."[20] In his first term as governor, Brown widely expanded state programs, such as infrastructure projects and newly established college campuses, using revenues generated by tax increases.[21] His supposed lack of responsible fiscal spending and inability to properly gauge public concern led conservatives to embrace an anti-statist critique of the Californian governor. Nixon affirmed, stating, "This will just be another example of the boondoggling with kited checks for which this administration is already famous."[22] For Republicans, Brown's expansive vision of California government prompted a conservative response. Republicans, Nixon believed, could uproot the continuation of Brown's liberal status quo.

A conservative vision of limited state governance continued to dominate the Republican platform in the 1966 gubernatorial race. Saying in 1967, "the road ahead to a better, more responsible, more meaningful life for all our citizens, a life in which they are allowed to develop and pursue their aims and ambitions to the fullest, without the constant interference and domination of big spending, big government," gubernatorial candidate Ronald Reagan forcefully characterized Brown's liberal and proactive style of state governance as intrusive.[23] He argued that Brown's liberal agenda was fundamentally unprogressive and impotent at solving societal issues. Reagan's conservatism assumed that liberalism had failed to provide Californians with the norms and values needed for society to flourish. Though Brown deemed liberalism a valuable progressive tool, conservatives labeled an expansive federal government as ineffective. Distinct differences in these visions intensified political disagreements and contributed to the establishment of rigidly opposed ideological principles.

Despite their differences, Brown and Reagan envisioned an America shaped by its unique values and institutions, where citizens could take risks, practice their faith, participate in their government, and be protected from intolerance. Nevertheless, Brown and Reagan supported these fundamental values with contrasting premises about state governance. Reagan promoted support for mainstream conservative values – such as limited state governance – in his campaign for governor, saying, "Along this path government will lead but not rule, listen but not lecture. It is the path of a Creative Society."[24] Reagan's outlook on state governance contrasted considerably with Brown's. Reagan articulated a belief in a constrained governing body checked by the power of the general public. His support for conservatism embodied a movement that viewed uncontained governmental authority as an attack on democracy and freedom. Brown cited Reagan's position as "extremist." Since his first term as governor, Brown had relied on his belief in progressive state governance. He argued that "extremists" had created Reagan's campaign plan and dismissed Reagan's "Creative Society" as a unsubstantive approach to state politics.[25] Although Reagan's rhetorical attack on Brown's liberal vision was not based upon far-right extremist ideals, Reagan did aim to dismantle Brown's expansion of California state governance. To Brown, Reagan's plan would undo the progressive vision his administration had embraced since 1958. The 1966 campaign showed the growing maneuvering of these ideologies through their interaction in the gubernatorial race.

The interactions between the Republican and Democratic parties led to the formulation of opposing sets of ideals for California society. By the late 1950s, liberalism defined a California government that aggressively dismantled structures of power that infringed upon the rights and freedoms of the state's citizens.[26] This egalitarian ethos was unique to Brown's liberalism. The culmination of ideas and policies under Brown allowed his governorship to successfully win a second term in 1962. For the first time in nearly twenty years, the manifestation of a liberal vision of California society outlined a new future for Californians. Nonetheless, Brown's vision of proactive state governance would generate vast discontent among conservatives.

During the early 1960s, liberal and conservative beliefs formulated rigid ideological principles that later defined party lines. To properly communicate these general principles to Californians, the Democratic and Republican parties formulated policy recommendations in the form of legislative proposals and executive actions. During the 1962 and 1966 gubernatorial elections, candidates running for office described, altered, and critiqued the beliefs of their electoral opponents.[27] Brown, Nixon, and then Reagan all conveyed their ideological beliefs in order to convince Californians to vote for their platforms. In both the 1962 and 1966 campaigns, pertinent and contested issues facing California, such as social welfare, racial discrimination, and unrest at the UC Berkeley campus, dictated the candidates' campaign rhetoric. The development of specific ideological tenets of liberal and conservative thought thus occurred during these gubernatorial campaigns.

Between 1958 and 1966, Governor Brown sought to limit rampant economic inequality through economic reform. By the end of his first term, Brown had increased spending on social welfare programs that aimed to alleviate economic hardship facing California's poorest residents.[28] He outlined this transformation in his second inaugural address saying, "Our social welfare programs place new emphasis on the principle that those receiving public assistance want a chance for honest work, not government charity for life."[29] His defense of California's social programs discredited conservative notions that disfavored expansive public spending on welfare. While campaigning against Reagan, Brown defended his stance by indicating that the election of a Republican governor would signify an end to social welfare programs.[30] Noting that Reagan aspired to end Social Security Programs, Brown said, "He got his start in ultraconservative politics fighting the aged in this country,"[31] programs established "under the banner of responsible liberalism." For Brown, conservative critiques on social programs were a direct attack on his egalitarian vision of California liberalism.[32]

Brown's approach to tackling economic inequality, not surprisingly, did not resonate well with conservative California Republicans. By 1966, Reagan's stance on government spending mostly mirrored the 1962 Nixon campaign's argument that government mismanagement had precipitated economic problems in the state. Reagan articulated this belief in a debate against Governor Brown less than a week before Election Day, arguing that government spending needed to consolidate unneeded waste by streamlining efficiency and by defunding programs that expanded welfare benefits.[33] Reagan's drift toward language that embraced fiscal responsibility targeted Brown's expansive policy measures that had increased state spending on welfare and other social programs. His disapproval of Brown's spending agenda resonated among conservatives, many of whom had expressed similar values earlier in the decade.

While Democratic and Republican platforms promoted conflicting policies on governmental spending, during the 1962 gubernatorial race, their platforms developed similar views on combating racial discrimination in California. During his tenure as governor, Brown based his liberal principles on the belief that all men and women, regardless of race, deserved equal access to employment and housing.[34] Citing President Lincoln's Emancipation Proclamation in his second inaugural address, Brown asked Californians to support his extension of laws prohibiting discrimination in housing and employment practices. To accomplish this policy, Brown intended to "wipe out all vestiges of discrimination in state government."[35] The role of Brown's liberalism in combating racial discrimination thus revolved around the use of governmental force to uproot discriminatory practices in the public and private sector.

Interestingly, Nixon's policy on race and discrimination mostly mirrored Brown's liberal platform. Preceding the passage of the Civil Rights Act of 1964 and Voting Rights Act of 1965, liberal and conservative policy recommendations articulated support for the dismantling of racially discriminatory structures in Californian society. Nixon, however, branded Brown's Fair Employment Practices Act as failing to address the discriminatory labor practices that he argued were occurring in Californian labor unions.[36] In a speech to African American voters, Nixon articulated the conservative stance as the position that took the "offensive against discrimination."[37] Though Brown positioned California's government as anti-discriminatory, Nixon asserted that his governorship would more effectively continue the legislative fight against racial prejudice and discrimination. By 1962, liberal and conservative policies both proposed utilizing state force to combat racial discrimination. Nonetheless, conservatives viewed racial discrimination as strictly a structural issue in society. Although their platform opposed overt racial prejudice and discrimination, their beliefs tended to ignore the social consequences of implicitly supporting racial discrimination. In their interaction, Republican and Democratic platforms framed racial discrimination as an issue arising out of different facets of Californian society.

Conservatism's policy towards racial discrimination, however, devolved during Reagan's campaign for governor. In 1965, the Watts Riots exacerbated racial tensions between white conservatives and African Americans, specifically in Los Angeles. Growing dissatisfaction in the black community materialized following the passage of the Voting Rights Act of 1965 and caused violent unrest in the Watts community and intensified resentment towards the Los Angeles Police Department.[38] The enactment of the 1964 Rumford Fair Housing Act, which took aim at combating racialized housing practices that denied renting or selling to racial minorities, broadened the ideological divide between conservative and liberal thought. Describing the Rumford Act as "a big brother sitting in Sacramento," Reagan hammered the liberal policy on the grounds that it caused white racial backlash.[39] Though the target of the legislation was simple, combating discriminatory housing practices, Reagan argued that the act "invaded one of our most basic and cherished rights – a right held by all of our citizens – the right to dispose of property to whom we see fit and as we see fit."[40] For conservatives, Reagan's preservation of property rights triumphed over the state's call for equal housing. His comments, however, heightened existing racial tensions in the state between black and white Californians. As governor, Reagan upheld the act due to its symbolic importance to the African American community.[41] Nonetheless, at the time, Reagan's staunch defense of property rights reflected the concerns white conservatives felt about Brown's enactment of the Rumsford Act and the social unrest occurring in South Central Los Angeles.

Ideological disagreement evolved along different fronts as Governor Brown outlined his support for the protection of academic freedom in California universities during the 1962 gubernatorial campaign. Brown was a staunch defender of public education. His belief in liberalism's duty to supply the general public with an adequate education led him to create the California state university system. While proposing legislative policy that would expand funding and lower tuition costs for higher education, Brown defended his ideological position, saying, "Our public schools have begun shoring up their curricula to meet the stern demands of an age in which the only public cost greater than education is ignorance."[42] Brown also directly referenced Nixon's policy that took aim at combatting communist influence in California higher education, saying, "The role he [Nixon] assigns himself – censor of books, inquisitor of teachers – is a clear violation of the Constitution of this state and of our California insistence on the independence of public education."[43] To Brown, his liberal platform embraced truly "American" norms that encouraged political dissent and freedom of thought.

Communism's perceived threat to the state's college population, nonetheless, dominated the development of conservative policy in the 1962 gubernatorial race.[44] When asked if alleged subversives should be permitted to speak at public universities, Nixon claimed, "Those who invoke the Fifth Amendment when asked by a grand jury or an investigating committee as to whether they are members of the Communist Party, should be barred from speaking on the campuses of tax-supported colleges and universities."[45] Nixon perceived Brown's policy on addressing communist influence in higher education as soft. Conservative Republicans instead vocalized support for a hard-line stance that directly combated any anti-American rhetoric or influence through governmental force. By the end of the 1962 campaign, the production of rigid ideological beliefs generated different policy recommendation regarding freedom of speech in the California higher education system.

By 1966, unrest at a prominent Californian university had expanded the ideological contrast between conservative and liberal platforms. In 1964, a group of students were jailed for protesting rules restricting political activity on the UC Berkeley campus. As their protest developed, demonstrations grew in size. In response the campus canceled academic activities, and Governor Brown responded by using police force to arrest demonstrators.[46] The debate over the Berkeley Free Speech Movement and the handling of protests at the university quickly became a central issue in the 1966 gubernatorial campaign and a defining interaction between liberal and conservative ideals.

While governor, Brown believed collegiate students had the authority and right to protest. Nonetheless, following the forceful occupation of a campus building, he ordered the Berkeley police to quell the student demonstrations. Brown's use of police force, however, was limited. He asked Berkeley police to "very gently tell them to get out [and] give them every chance in the world, right down to the last minute," to conclude the protests.[47] Brown believed this was an appropriate response to the demonstrations. Brown's hesitation to disregard his idealistic beliefs damaged his ability to look tough in power, which allowed conservatives to question his leadership and the validity of his liberal values.

In failing to quickly end the protests, Brown's leadership and liberal values came under conservative attack. In response, Reagan positioned conservatism as the ideology that supported the importance of rules. While campaigning, Reagan characterized the Berkeley students' movement as "a small minority of beatniks, radicals and filthy speech advocates" that "have brought great shame on a great university."[48] According to Reagan, Brown's failure to quickly quell the student protests reflected liberalism's inability to resolve the supposed moral degradation and unrest occurring throughout the state.[49] Conservatism, to Reagan, emphasized the importance of maintaining the rules, structures, and regulations that made California's collegiate institutions great. Reagan articulated his position, saying,

> We are proud of our ability to provide this opportunity for our youth and we believe it is no denial of academic freedom to provide this education within a framework of reasonable rules and regulations. Nor is it a violation of individual rights to require obedience to these rules and regulations.

Conservative ideals thus emerged in response to Brown's perceived inaction towards the Berkeley student protests. Reagan's hawkish approach to quelling the demonstrations illustrated a key conservative talking point in the 1966 gubernatorial election.

Reagan thus promoted the importance of social obedience and positioned conservatism as the party of "law and order." Citing the presence of a leadership gap, Reagan affirmed his belief that advocates of the Berkeley Free Speech Movement should have been "taken by the scruff of the neck and thrown out of the university once and for all."[50] Conservatism's response to liberal inaction during the Berkeley Free Speech Movement marked a contrasting approach to solving societal unrest. Reagan's rhetoric regarding social instability offered a hard-line stance on political dissent that stood in contrast to Brown's alleged failures with the Berkeley Free Speech Movement. As governor, Reagan regarded his response to such protests as "lawlessness by the mob, as with the individual, will not be tolerated." Reagan continued, "We will act firmly and quickly to put down riot or insurrection wherever and whenever the situation requires."[51] Though Reagan only used the National Guard once during his tenure as governor, his early policy ideas reflected a political environment profoundly affected by external events.[52] The Berkeley Free Speech Movement and the Watts Riots occurred during a time period of liberal state and national governance. Events like these provided Californian conservatism platforms from which to critique Governor Brown's liberal agenda and formulate an alternate pragmatic political pathway.

These significant differences in political policy produced increasingly distinct state political parties. Reoccurring issues facing California forced liberals and conservatives to articulate their beliefs and work to persuade Californians to adopt their political principles. Although these ideals most visibly manifest themselves in California's gubernatorial elections, they also garnered immense influence on the future of national politics.

Under the pressure of gubernatorial races, public opinion, and ideological foes, Democratic and Republican Party platforms formulated conflicting visions of American society that placed contrasting importance on the authority of the government and the role of the populace. These visions dictated the development and articulation of the ideological principles and policies that each party would create while campaigning for gubernatorial office. While discussing pertinent issues then facing society, the engineering of these ideologies formed rigid beliefs that dictated Republican and Democratic policies on fiscal spending, protest culture, and the implementation of anti-discrimination legislation. Under the guidance of their ideological principles, candidates such as Edmund Brown, Richard Nixon, and Ronald Reagan strived to obtain an electoral majority and implement their policy agendas.

Ideological interaction is an important ongoing process that allows our society to evolve and produce nuanced ideas on contemporary issues. Although their development occurred nearly sixty years ago, California conservative and liberal platforms directly addressed issues that are still pressing today. Their combination of new and old ideas amplified their importance as trendsetters for national politics. Following Nixon's electoral loss in 1962, he would be elected president in 1968. Moreover, within twenty years of Reagan's gubernatorial victory he would become president of the United States. Today, American political thought is defined to a diverse set of beliefs, values, and ideas that reflect the transformative development of California liberalism and conservatism during the 1960s.

Notes

1. Lisa McGirr, *Suburban Warriors: The Origins of the New American Right* (Princeton: Princeton University Press, 2001), 21.
2. Ethan Rarick, *California Rising: The Life and Times of Pat Brown* (Berkeley: University of California Press, 2005), 108.
3. Jonathan Bell, *California Crucible: The Forging of Modern American Liberalism*

(Philadelphia: University of Pennsylvania Press, 2012); Matthew Dallek, *The Right Movement: Ronald Reagan's First Victory and the Decisive Turning Point in American Politics* (New York: Free Press, 2000); Kurt Schuparra, *Triumph of the Right: The Rise of the California Conservative Movement, 1945–1966* (Armonk: M. E. Sharpe, 1998); Rarick, *California Rising*; McGirr, *Suburban Warriors*; Gerald J De Groot, "'A Goddamned Electable Person': The 1966 California Gubernatorial Campaign of Ronald Reagan," *History* 82 (July 1997): 429–48.

4. Bell, *California Crucible*, 124.
5. Jonathan Bell, "Social Democracy and the Rise of the Democratic Party in California, 1950–1964," *The Historical Journal* 49 (June 2006): 499–501.
6. Bell, *California Crucible*, 141.
7. McGirr, *Suburban Warriors*, 70–71.
8. McGirr, *Suburban Warriors*, 68–69.
9. McGirr, *Suburban Warriors*, 119–21.
10. Rarick, *California Rising*, 242.
11. Rarick, *California Rising*, 251–56.
12. Schuparra, *Triumph of the Right*, 102.
13. Schuparra, *Triumph of the Right*, 118.
14. Rarick, *The Life and Times of Pat Brown*, 358–61.
15. Edmund G. Brown, "First Inaugural Address," January 5, 1959, The Governor's Gallery, http://governors.library.ca.gov/addresses/32-Pbrown01.html (accessed March 31, 2019).
16. Brown, "First Inaugural Address."
17. Brown, "First Inaugural Address."
18. Schuparra, *Triumph of the Right*, 149–52.
19. Schuparra, *Triumph of the Right*, 59–61.
20. Los Angeles Times News Service, "Nixon Isn't Team Player, Brown Says," *Los Angeles Times*, October 1, 1962, 2.
21. Rarick, *The Life and Times of Pat Brown*, 229.
22. Carl Greenberg, "Nixon Charges Brown Considers Tax Boosts," *Los Angeles Times*, October 5, 1962, 2.
23. Ronald Reagan, "Address by Governor Ronald Reagan," May 6, 1967, Ronald Reagan Presidential Library, https://www.reaganlibrary.gov/research/speeches/05061967a (accessed March 31, 2019).
24. Ronald Reagan, "Inaugural Address," January 5, 1967.
25. Richard Bergholz, "'Extremist' Created Reagan's Campaign Plan, Brown Claims," *Los Angeles Times*, October 13, 1966, 3.
26. Brown, "First Inaugural Address."
27. Bell, *California Crucible*, 169.
28. Edmund G. Brown, "Second Inaugural Address," January 7, 1963, The Governor's Gallery, http://governors.library.ca.gov/addresses/32-Pbrown02.html (accessed March 31, 2019).
29. Brown, "Second Inaugural Address."
30. Jerry Gillam, "Wealthy Birch Society Member Backs Reagan, Brown Says," *Los Angeles Times*, October 11, 1966, 3.
31. Richard Bergholz, "Reagan Opposes Aid for Elderly, Brown Declares," *Los Angeles*

Times, October 17, 1966, 3.
32. Brown, "Second Inaugural Address."
33. Ronald Reagan and Edmund Brown, "1966 California Governor's Forum Ronald Reagan & Edmund 'Pat' Brown – Preview," November 3, 1966, in American History TV C-SPAN3, Youtube, https://www.youtube.com/watch?v=442rW8QaRtA (accessed March 31, 2019).
34. Brown, "Second Inaugural Address."
35. Brown, "Second Inaugural Address."
36. Richard Bergholz, "Negro Voters Hear Nixon from Pulpit," *Los Angeles Times,* October 22, 1962, 2.
37. Bergholz, "Negro Voters Hear Nixon from Pulpit."
38. David Farber and Beth Bailey, *The Columbia Guide to America in the 1960s* (New York: Columbia University Press, 2001), 254–55.
39. "Rumford Act Breeds Bitterness – Reagan," *Los Angeles Times,* October 7, 1966, 3.
40. "Rumford Act Breeds Bitterness – Reagan," 3.
41. Jackson K. Putnam, "Governor Reagan: A Reappraisal," *California History* 83, no. 5 (2006): 27–29.
42. Brown, "Second Inaugural Address."
43. Carl Greenberg, "Nixon Wants to Become Dictator, Brown Charges in Tough Speech," *Los Angeles Times,* October 10, 1962, 2.
44. Rarick, *California Rising,* 242–44.
45. Richard Bergholz, "Nixon Accuses Gov. Brown of Vilifying Him," *Los Angeles Times,* October 11, 1962, 2.
46. Rarick, *California Rising,* 2.
47. Bensch and Saeed, "Interview with Pat Brown," October 13, 1978, Media Resources Center Collection, University of California, https://archive.org/details/cabe-mrc_00002 (accessed April 17, 2019).
48. Ronald Reagan, "'Morality Gap' Speech," May 12, 1966, Bay Area Television Archive, https://diva.sfsu.edu/collections/sfbatv/bundles/229317 (accessed March 31, 2019).
49. Michelle Reeves, "'Obey the Rules or Get Out': Ronald Reagan's 1966 Gubernatorial Campaign and the 'Trouble in Berkeley,'" *Southern California Quarterly* 93, no. 3 (Fall 2010): 277.
50. Reagan, "'Morality Gap' Speech."
51. Reagan, "Inaugural Address."
52. Lou Cannon, *Governor Reagan* (New York: PublicAffairs, 2003), 292.

2. John F. Kennedy: A Man of the People

ABIGAIL SIMKO

On November 22, 1963, the world stood still. A seemingly average day quickly turned tragic as the words "John F. Kennedy is dead" appeared on television broadcasts and newspaper headlines across the world. America's president was taken from the world in Dallas after he was shot during a motorcade by Lee Harvey Oswald. The man that the people elected to be president was killed one year before his term was supposed to end, leaving the nation devastated.

A Boston native, Kennedy began his political journey when he became a representative of Massachusetts in 1945 and then a senator in 1953. He and his wife, Jacqueline (Jackie), with their two young children, quickly became a symbol of the ideal postwar American family, while their elegance led many to refer to the Kennedys as a kind of modern-day Camelot. John Kennedy was a different type of presidential candidate who seemed to be exactly what the country wanted during the 1960 election.

President Kennedy came into office at a time when the United States was facing many challenges. America was still recovering from the Korean War, which had ended seven years prior, but communism was still spreading. The threat of nuclear war was still present, and tensions with the U.S.S.R. continued to grow every day. On the home front, racism was strong and the fight for equality was still being fought. The pressure of being the first president of the 1960s was enormous, but those pressures did not deter Kennedy.

Other historians have commented on the way America viewed JFK during his presidency. Many Americans thought of him as the modern president who would help them through the difficult times of the 1960s. While some historians criticize him for the different things he did while in office, such as the escalation of the Vietnam War and the approval of several assassination attempts on Cuban leader Fidel Castro, these were revelations that came out after his untimely death. According to one historian, these disclosures, as well as other disclosures that regarded his personal life, were not reported and written about until the 1970s and 1980s.[1] When these books and articles did come out, they revealed inside information about Berlin, the Bay of Pigs invasion, the Cuban Missile Crisis, and the burgeoning war in Vietnam. President Kennedy's plans and feelings towards these issues were revealed to the public for the first time, and that is when the shift in public opinion towards Kennedy occurred. However, these publications do not reveal how the public felt about President Kennedy while he was in office, or even immediately after his assassination.[2]

This chapter explores how Americans viewed Kennedy at the time of his presidency, without any of the knowledge that they might have acquired years after his passing. Did the nation have as much faith in him when he announced his plan to run for the presidency? Once his presidency began, did the support for him ever waiver? How did people remember him after he was killed? Exploring the answers to these questions will provide a better understanding of how the nation felt about John F. Kennedy and how those feelings were affected by the different events of his presidency, both at home and overseas.

John F. Kennedy played a hugely influential role in the history of the sixties, and his assassination affected the way that the rest of the decade went. Lyndon B. Johnson used Kennedy as a tool to get the nation on his side and push his political agenda forward. For a president to have that much influence on the American people has been extremely difficult to achieve since Kennedy, but it was something Kennedy seemed able to do with ease. While John F. Kennedy experienced difficulties throughout his candidacy and presidency, the American people rarely swayed and continued to have an unwavering support for him that lasted throughout the years that followed his assassination.

Before

President Eisenhower was in office for eight years, and his term would come to an end in 1961. This would allow a new candidate the opportunity to take his place; but the question was who. President Eisenhower's vice president, Richard Nixon, stepped up and became the obvious choice for the Republican Party. On January 2, 1960, a candidate stepped forward that would end up having a lasting effect on the nation: John F. Kennedy. In the Senate Caucus Room in Washington, D.C., Senator Kennedy announced his nomination and vowed to find solutions for the important issues of the time. This declaration would lead to mixed reactions across the nation.[3]

While this announcement did not come as a surprise to many in Washington, D.C., it officially put Kennedy in the race. The news stirred multiple opinions in the nation, and some of those opinions conveyed support and excitement for Kennedy. He was not the only Democrat in the race, and he faced competition against men like Hubert Humphrey, Lyndon Johnson, Stuart Symington, and Adlai Stevenson – four men who were not going to make the candidacy easy for Kennedy. While Kennedy was young and wide-eyed, he did have several things working against him.[4]

The biggest setback he faced was his religion. Kennedy was a Roman Catholic, and he was the first Roman Catholic to run for office since 1951. During that earlier election, the candidate dropped out due to anti-Catholic prejudice, a decision some were afraid Kennedy would make as well.[5] The issue of Kennedy's religion came from the idea of separation of church and state, and the fear that if he was elected, that separation would come to an end. In 1928, New York governor Alfred E. Smith was on the presidential ballot, and he was a Catholic. His campaign was destroyed because of this fact, and many even went on to say that "he would build a tunnel from the White House to the Vatican."[6] Although the nation evolved from the 1920s to the 1960s, the idea of having a Catholic president still scared the nation. Americans were afraid that faith would infiltrate the White House and affect the decisions that the president would make.

Virginia and West Virginia voters had a particularly hard time accepting Kennedy's religion. Once Kennedy's nomination was confirmed and he became the Democrat on the 1960 presidential election ticket, many churches in Virginia (and the South as a whole) began speaking out against Senator Kennedy because of his religious views. One article in *The Washington Post* observed that "there is a deep-seated distrust of Catholicism. In the southside and the southwest mountains the ministers are speaking out from the pulpits against the election of a Catholic."[7] West Virginia also showed a deep-rooted bias against Catholics. When Kennedy first entered the West Virginia primaries, he was behind by 20 points, which could be in direct relation to the fact that Catholics made up less than 4% of the population of the state.[8] People who put a lot of stake in their religion tended to just see the fact that Kennedy was Catholic, and their differing religious beliefs tended to influence the way that they voted. The religious bias ran so deep that Kennedy had whole churches voting against him in this election.

The South tended to be a tough spot for Senator Kennedy's campaign. In addition to Kennedy's religion, his views on civil rights caused Southern Democrats to have major doubts about the Massachusetts native. Jim Crow and discrimination were in full force throughout the South in the early sixties, and part of Kennedy's campaign was to work towards racial equality in America. During his campaign, Kennedy worked to assist in the release of civil rights activist Dr. Martin Luther King Jr. from prison when King was arrested in Atlanta, Georgia, for protesting. This aligned himself with the fight for civil rights but also put a wedge between him and white Southern Democratic voters.[9] When his nomination got confirmed by the Democratic National Convention, the people of Dallas expressed their concerns by saying that "the conservatives will find Kennedy more liberal then the candidate they had hoped for" and "Kennedy will have difficulty holding the 'Solid South' – both because of the strong civil rights plank adopted over Southern protest."[10] The country was divided on this issue, and Kennedy's stance on civil rights caused the South to be hesitant about his nomination.

While the South was skeptical about Kennedy's nomination, there were those who urged the nation to look past the superficial bias against Kennedy and focus on electing the best president for the nation. As stated earlier, when Kennedy first announced that he was running for president, some expressed concern over his Catholicism. Many also jumped to his defense. In an article written in *The Washington Post* by an anonymous writer, the author defended Kennedy and his religion and stated that Kennedy should be welcomed by people of all religious faiths and "should be judged only on his capacity for national leadership."[11] Vice President Nixon echoed this statement as the election neared by saying, "We need the best man that America can produce, regardless of his party label, regardless of his religion, regardless of any other factor."[12] The words of Nixon and the anonymous writer urged the nation to focus on what mattered, and that was getting the best president the nation could have.

Most of the country seemed to take the advice of the *The Washington Post* and of Vice President Nixon. Kennedy's religious beliefs did not seem to hinder him in the primaries as much as the country might have thought. In the polls, Kennedy seemed to pull ahead of the other Democratic possibilities. In June of 1960, Gallup asked 3,393 country chairmen of both the Democratic and Republican party, "Regardless of who you personally prefer, what is your best guess at this time as to who actually will get the Democratic nomination for President in 1960?" The options were Kennedy, Johnson, Symington, Stevenson, and "Others." The results of this poll showed Kennedy pulled 51% of the Democratic chairmen's support and 41% of the Republican chairmen's support. Johnson came in second, only pulling 18% of the Democratic votes and 26% of the Republican votes. As for who the Democrats wanted to see as the Democratic candidate, Kennedy only pulled 34% of the votes, with Johnson pulling 28%. While Kennedy was only the personal choice by a small margin, he was the man that both Democrats and Republicans felt would be the 1960 presidential candidate to go up against GOP front-runner Vice President Nixon.[13]

This confidence in Kennedy spanned many different areas of the country. After the Democratic National Convention, different newspapers had extremely positive things to say about Kennedy and his chances against the Republican candidate, Richard Nixon. A newspaper out of Washington, D.C., said that "Democrats at Los Angeles have nominated their strongest contender for the Presidency," and *The Chicago Daily News* was quoted saying, "The organizing ability Kennedy showed is fair warning to the Republican party that it faces a very stiff fall campaign." Seattle even commented on Kennedy and his Roman Catholic beliefs by saying, "Kennedy's nomination not only is a tribute to his dynamic personal qualities but is meaningful in many other respects. Not the least of these is the decline of religious prejudice as a factor in American politics." The support for Kennedy spanned from the East Coast to the West, but that did not mean Kennedy didn't face any backlash. The *St. Louis Post Dispatch* said that Kennedy was the best vote-getter, but not necessarily the best candidate for the job. Another newspaper that criticized the Democratic candidate was *The Los Angeles Times*. They said, "There is a ruthless, all's-well-in-love-and-politics quality in Kennedy's drive for the nomination and one cannot be sure yet whether it is the game that he loves or the candle that he deserves." Love for Kennedy was not unanimous across the entire nation, but many people were optimistic about Kennedy's chances against Nixon, making the 1960 election one to watch.[14]

This support continued through the rest of his campaign, but on Election Day the results were anything but clear. While Kennedy was able to gain the loyalty of the many different parts of the country, Vice President Nixon also had a great amount of backing. Final counts had Kennedy at 49.7% of the votes and Nixon having 49.5% of the votes, leaving the margins minuscule. The doubts that the nation had about the young senator were evident in the election. By only 100,000 votes out of over 68 million votes, Senator Kennedy became President-Elect Kennedy.[15]

John F. Kennedy came from the Senate and ended up being the man that would lead the nation in its difficulties and help bring the nation through the Cold War. Despite his religious preferences, he was still able to gain the country's trust and become the man that would be president. With the second leading Democrat, Lyndon B. Johnson, at his side as vice president, victory was able to find him, even if it was a victory that was not easily won. With the support of the public, Kennedy was able to sneak past Nixon and secure the White House as the first president of the decade.

During

The public support that Kennedy received during his campaign foreshadowed how he would be perceived during the rest of his presidency. The majority of the country was excited and optimistic about the Kennedy administration and continued to show support throughout his presidency. The 1960s was a decade filled with global and domestic tension, and Kennedy was elected as the man to help ease that tension. Kennedy was able to keep the support of the people throughout his presidency, especially with the help of his policies and his family.

Despite the extremely small margin of Kennedy's win in 1960, he was still able to enter the presidency with a lot of support from the American people and from the world. He won on a platform that included civil rights as well as the intention of ending the Cold War – all issues that resonated with the

American public. It was his stance on the Cold War, in particular, that got the attention of the rest of the world. Kennedy fought for the presidency, understanding the issues and tensions that came with the nuclear race between the United States and the Soviet Union. He understood that his Soviet counterpart, Khrushchev, was building up his missile supply, and Kennedy vowed to do what he needed to do to prevent nuclear war.[16] Just weeks after his inauguration, Kennedy was polled as more favorable than Khrushchev in four other large nations. In West Germany, Kennedy was found to be highly favored by 45% of the people and mildly favorable by 27% of the people. This meant that he was overall favored by 72% of the population, Khrushchev only being favored by 10% of the population. Kennedy's favorability was also shown in Holland, where he was favored by 62% of the nation over Khrushchev's 11% favor rating. Johannesburg echoed the rest of the world, with Kennedy reaching 69% of the country's favor, while Khrushchev only had 9%.[17] Kennedy's views on the Cold War and nuclear weapons seemed to resonate with people in other parts of the world.

President Kennedy had the ability to use the problems abroad to foster support in his own country. When Kennedy was in office, he created the Peace Corps, which still sends volunteers to different underdeveloped countries to help in any way that they can. The Peace Corps' mission is to "immerse themselves in a community abroad, working side by side with the local leaders to tackle the most pressing challenges of our generation."[18] Kennedy would frequently visit the original members of the Peace Corps to show his support for them. During one of his visits he said, "Americans should appreciate you because you are willing to leave your homes and go to these countries."[19] He would talk directly to the people who were helping his causes, and he would make them feel heard and feel important. By doing this, Kennedy was able to solidify the support of the people who participated in this organization and their families, which allowed those people to continue to work and make the world a better place.

His numbers at home showed his favor just as much as they did across the world. Kennedy had a way of speaking to the people and making them feel as if they could trust him. During his campaign, the American people got to see televised debates for the first time, so Kennedy's personality was able to shine through to the American people. His personality continued to shine when he took office, and people continued to react positively to it. When talking to the press and briefing them on the happenings of the country, one article said that "he has saved the conference news of real importance and has related it in an interesting, informative way. ... He appears well briefed on the details of what is going on. He remembers precisely which one among his newly selected associates he has instructed to do what."[20] Kennedy was able to gain support early on by being able to answer questions in a way that would keep the press and the country on his side.

Kennedy was also able to gain the support of the nation through its failures. In the the Cold War of the early 1960s, Americans lived in fear of the U.S.S.R. One thing that frightened the country was the idea of a nuclear weapon heading for America from the Soviet Union. To make matters worse, the Soviet Union was able to send an aircraft into space before America was, which made the nuclear threat even more daunting. America tried to keep up, but suffered failure after failure when it came to the Space Race. Kennedy's rhetoric, however, provided a silver lining for the American people when the outcome seemed grim and as if America would never catch up to the Soviets. He said to the American people, "We do not intend on staying behind, but we will make up for it and move ahead."[21] These words reassured the public and made the road ahead seem less daunting. Kennedy's optimism calmed the fears of the American people, allowing them to give Kennedy the support he needed.

The president was not the only member of the Kennedy family that dazzled the American people. The first lady, Jackie Kennedy, quickly became a popular favorite. She was young and many considered her to be very beautiful; she immediately became a "smash hit." From the very beginning, she decided to do things her own way, from how she decorated the White House to how she entertained different dignitaries in the building. She did things with style, and the American people loved it.[22]

Many Americans looked at her as not only a lovable First Lady, but as a fashion icon and loving mother. People viewed the Kennedy family as the "all-American family." The family took holidays together, and Jackie and John seemed like a loving and caring couple. One article recalls the family cruising on the Nantucket Sound, surrounded by friends and family. Mrs. Kennedy was seen in the water and swimming with other guests, and the Kennedy children were seen playing with the other children on the boat.[23] This image allowed American citizens to feel comfortable with the First Family and therefore with the president. They may have been "Camelot," but they went on vacations with their children and did things that average American families might be able to relate to. The relatability of the president and of his family permitted the American people to trust and support the president and the decisions he would make.

Despite having a picture-perfect family and endless public support, Kennedy was not able to keep everyone from questioning his decisions. In 1962, Republican senator Barry Goldwater of Arizona brought up the fact that Kennedy might be making secret deals with Premier Khrushchev regarding Cuba and missiles that were being stored there. Prior to this, it was discovered that the U.S.S.R. was storing missiles in Cuba and they were at a distance that could easily strike any major city in the United States. This worried many of the American people because nuclear war seemed closer than ever. Kennedy placed a naval blockade around Cuba and demanded that the U.S.S.R. remove its nuclear weapons immediately; in return, America promised to remove its nuclear weapons from Turkey. After thirteen days, the U.S.S.R. removed its nuclear missiles from Cuba, and America appeared to be in the clear once more, but Goldwater did not seem convinced.[24] Goldwater said that there was no indication that the Soviet missiles were removed or that the U.S.S.R. planned to pull its troops off the island. An article in the Los Angeles Times quoted Goldwater saying, "It's obvious he's ducking. I suspect from the way he's been using the press to regulate opinion this is only adding to the apprehension of Americans that all is not well in Cuba." This made Kennedy look less trustworthy and unlike the man that Americans elected two years prior.[25]

The tensions in Cuba led to a drop in support for the president, but it was not the sole reason for this dampening of support. Throughout his presidency, Kennedy had an average approval rating of 70% from 1961 to 1963.[26] While that is a high overall rating, his presidency did experience some drops and dips in mid-1963. A newspaper article claims that his support had dipped due to the civil rights crisis the country then faced. Kennedy continued to work with Dr. Martin Luther King Jr. on equality for both black and white citizens.[27] While black Americans were delighted with the way the issue was being dealt with, many white citizens were not pleased with Kennedy's approach, which caused his support and favor with the people to decrease to a 59% approval rating.[28] Civil rights was a sore spot for Kennedy during his campaign, and it continued to be a deterrent for his approval ratings as president.

Kennedy started his presidency on a high note after his election. The people were excited for the young president to come into the White House and lead the country. That excitement, however, might have dimmed, but it never completely burned out. The country continued to see the man that they elected, someone who had new ideas and was going to take the country to a new level. While he might not have been able to completely ease the stress that was ever present in the world, he was able to put the country's mind at ease enough to maintain over 50% of the support of the country. With his family by his side, John F. Kennedy seemed like he was going to be an unstoppable president for the remainder of his presidential term.

After

The day started out like any other. President Kennedy was in Dallas, Texas, participating in an open-car motorcade, and the square was filled with people. At 12:30 p.m., gunshots were fired and hit the president, putting an end to his life. The culprit, Lee Harvey Oswald, was caught on the same day that the new president, Lyndon B. Johnson, was sworn into office. Everything happened so fast, and within a moment, the First Lady lost her husband and the United States lost its beloved leader.[29]

President Johnson had to go from vice president to president in a matter of minutes. Kennedy was well-loved, and now Johnson was expected to lead the nation. The country was grieving and needed a way to move on from the tragedy that occurred. Johnson knew about the struggle of the American people and addressed it directly in the first speech he gave as president. This speech was given on November 27, 1963, just five days after the assassination. In this speech, Johnson said, "Today John Fitzgerald Kennedy lives on in the immortal words and works that he left behind." Johnson also addressed the new responsibility that had been given to him because of Oswald by saying, "An assassin's bullet has thrust upon me the awesome burden of the Presidency. I am here today to say I need your help; I cannot bear this burden alone." Johnson was able to use his own grief to connect with the public and help gain their support while also helping them grieve.[30]

Johnson knew that for his own presidency to be a successful one, he needed the people to remember Kennedy and the support they had for him. The hope was that it would then be transferred over to him. In one article from the time, the author stated that Johnson would have been unable to get the administration he needed for his presidency without Kennedy's assassination, and with the assassination being so recent, Kennedy's administration was more than willing to stand by Johnson's side. The mantra was "It's what Jack would have wanted." The author also said that "in his drive for election in his own right next November, Johnson's single greatest asset [was] the memory of his predecessor." This tragedy ended up being the driving force of the first part of Johnson's presidency and was the main cause of most of the support he received.[31]

While Johnson tried to get the nation to rally behind him, it was clear that the American public still preferred the late president over its current one. Johnson was unable to gain the support that Kennedy had, and once Johnson was able to push through the remainder of Kennedy's agenda, the nation was less interested in Johnson's presidency. In a poll taken in 1966, five to one Americans said that they felt Kennedy was a better president than Johnson. It also showed that most Americans preferred Robert Kennedy to be president over Johnson, in large part because he had the Kennedy name. The name Kennedy alone was enough to make the people excited about the possibilities. Johnson was able to create a martyr out of John Kennedy, but the mantle of martyrdom was not able to carry Johnson through his presidency.[32]

Kennedy had been a symbol of hope for the nation, and his family had been a picture of what the ideal American family looked like. Suddenly, Americans were missing their symbol and seeing pictures and videos of this family grieving. One photo struck a chord with many Americans. As Kennedy's body was being carried down the street, his son Jack Jr., who was only three, saluted his father's coffin as it passed.[33] The photographer said that this photo was "the saddest thing I've ever seen in my whole life." Much of the nation also felt this way. Here was a three-year-old boy who had just lost his father, and instead of crying he was saluting him. While he might not have known it, he was showing his father the ultimate sign of respect. The nation could relate to this photo, and it was one that continued to uphold the legacy of Kennedy and the respect that the nation had for him.[34]

The respect for Kennedy continued beyond his son's salute. One year after his assassination, the country still spoke about Kennedy in the highest regards. The mayor of Detroit, Jerome Cavanaugh, said that "God gave this gifted man but a few moments to contribute his vast abilities to history. ... We shall never forget this man." An anonymous author in the *San Francisco News-Call Bulletin* praised the late president by saying, "Mr. Kennedy was a personality of rare style and spirit. Never has such dash and wit graced the White House." These quotes show that Kennedy was beloved. Even one year after his death, he was still seen in the same high regard that he was held in during his time in office.[35]

Kennedy was beloved because he did something that the country desperately needed – he gave the people confidence, a confidence that the nation continued to associate with his name. This became easier for the nation to do because of President Kennedy's brother Robert. Robert Kennedy (RFK) was able to provide a consistent reassurance that the late president's spirit would still be with America. When asked about his brother, Robert Kennedy said he "gave us all more confidence in the country" and "he made Americans feel young again." Robert was there to remind the country why they loved President Kennedy in the first place, and he was able to keep that love alive, even after his death. He was also able to give the country updates on the former First Lady. In regard to Mrs. Kennedy, Robert said, "She's fine, really, and making an adjustment and doing it well. She spends most all of her time with her children." Robert Kennedy allowed the world to continue to view the Kennedys as a pillar of the nation and in a way that would continue to make them feel confident when hearing the Kennedy name.[36]

That confidence continued to carry the Kennedy name in high regard after the assassination. The nation was polled two years after the assassination of President Kennedy, and 40% of Americans said that the event was the thing that they were most ashamed of in this country. The way that blacks were treated came in second place with 21%. Also, 66% of the nation said that the assassination was something they still often felt bad about. This shows how impactful the death of Kennedy was even two years after the fact. The country still loved and admired him and viewed his death as being worse than issues like racial inequality or the burgeoning war in Vietnam. Kennedy left an impact on the people that even death couldn't erase.[37]

The death of Kennedy was a national tragedy and was something that took the people time to get over, but that does not mean that the support for Kennedy wavered in any way. Kennedy was still beloved by the people, and very few spoke ill of him and the decisions that he made. The nation saw him as a national martyr and as a symbol of hope for the country. Johnson used this symbol to get the people to rally behind him and as a way to get legislation passed. As a country, the people were able to grieve him and look to figures such as Robert Kennedy and President Johnson as reassurance that everything was going to be okay. This caused the nation to look at President Kennedy, and the former First Family, as strong and unwavering, exactly the thing the nation needed.

Conclusion

When most people list their top presidents, many still list John F. Kennedy as their number one choice. He was the very first president of the sixties, and he was one of the most charismatic people to step foot in the White House. The American people loved him and supported him until the very end of his life. The average approval rating during his administration was the highest that it has ever been for American presidents, at 70%, and the way the people felt about it makes it clear why that was the way it was.

When Kennedy ran for president, the public got to see him in a way that they had never seen presidential candidates before: through televised debates. This allowed Americans to see his personality, which ended up being a driving factor during the election. He was personable, and the American people felt as if they could trust him just by looking at him. After a hard-fought campaign, Kennedy was able to come out the winner of the 1960 election by extremely narrow margins against Richard Nixon.

During his presidency, Kennedy continued to hold the support of the American people consistently. The Kennedy family became the perfect picture of American families, and his wife gave women a reason to pay attention to the

First Family and, therefore, become more encouraged to vote for Kennedy and to pledge their support to him. While he did have his difficulties in office with the Soviet Union and Cuba, he was still able to maintain the support of over half of the nation. While it is hard to say for certain, there is no reason to believe that he would not have won reelection if he was given the chance.

Kennedy was never given the chance to run for reelection because his life was taken from him far too soon by an assassination. After his death, the country continued to hold a great amount of support for Kennedy. Johnson helped that happen by using Kennedy as a martyr for his own presidency. President Kennedy's brother was also able to help by providing encouraging words about the late president and his widowed wife, allowing the people to continue to associate strong people with the Kennedy name.

Support for President Kennedy was never something that the country was lacking. Time would go on, and the citizens of the United States continue to remember Kennedy in an extremely positive light. This just shows how much the nation has changed since Kennedy was in office, but also how much Kennedy truly meant to the people. Whether they supported him for his policies or because of the way he was taken from this earth, John F. Kennedy had a way about him that caused many to love him and many to give him their support.

Notes

1. Mark J. White, "Introduction: A New Synthesis for the New Frontier," in *Kennedy: The New Frontier Revisited* (New York: New York University Press, 1998), 1–15.
2. For more information on this, please see: Rebecca Friedman, "Crisis Management at the Dead Center: The 1960–1961 Presidential Transition and the Bay of Pigs Fiasco," *Presidential Studies Quarterly* 41, no. 2 (June 2011): 307–33; Mark Haefele, "John F. Kennedy, USIA, and World Public Opinion," *Diplomatic History* 25, no. 1 (Winter 2001): 63–84; Sidney Kraus, *Televised Presidential Debates and Public Policy*, 2nd ed., LEA's Communication Series (Mahwah, N.J.: Routledge, 2000); William J. Rust, *So Much to Lose: John F. Kennedy and American Policy in Laos* (Lexington: University Press of Kentucky, 2014); Larry Sabato, *The Kennedy Half-Century: The Presidency, Assassination, and Lasting Legacy of John F. Kennedy* (New York: Bloomsbury USA, 2013); Michael Schuyler, "Ghosts in the White House: LBJ, RFK and the Assassination of JFK," *Presidential Studies Quarterly* 17, no. 3 (Summer 1987): 503–18; Tom Smith, "Trends: The Cuban Missile Crisis and the U.S. Public Opinion," *The Public Opinion Quarterly* 67, no. 2 (Summer 2003):

265–93.
3. John F. Kennedy, "Statement of Senator John F. Kennedy Announcing his Candidacy for the Presidency of the United States," speech, Washington, D.C., January 4, 1960, JFK Library, https://www.jfklibrary.org/archives/other-resources/john-f-kennedy-speeches/presidential-candidacy-19600102 (accessed March 20, 2019).
4. George Gallup, "Country Chairmen See Kennedy-Nixon Contest," *Washington Post, Times Herald*, June 24, 1960, A2.
5. Church Seen, "Curb on Kennedy," *New York Times*, January 28, 1960, 20.
6. "John F. Kennedy and Religion: Anti-Catholic Prejudice Was Still Very Much in the Mainstream of American Life When JFK Decided to Seek the Presidency in 1960," JFK Library, https://www.jfklibrary.org/learn/about-jfk/jfk-in-history/john-f-kennedy-and-religion (accessed April 14, 2019).
7. Elsie Carper, "Virginia Called Kennedy's Weakest Spot in South," *Washington Post, Times Herald*, October 3, 1960.
8. "John F. Kennedy and Religion: West Virginia Primary," JFK Library, https://www.jfklibrary.org/learn/about-jfk/jfk-in-history/john-f-kennedy-and-religion (accessed April 14, 2019).
9. "Campaign of 1960: Television, Religion, and Civil Rights," JFK Library, https://www.jfklibrary.org/learn/about-jfk/jfk-in-history/campaign-of-1960 (accessed April 14, 2019).
10. "Editorial Opinion on Kennedy Victory," *New York Times*, July 15, 1960, 11.
11. "Senator Kennedy's Bid," *Washington Post, Times Herald*, January 4, 1960, A10.
12. Richard Nixon quoted in Willard Edwards, "Rejects Faith Issue," *Chicago Daily Tribune*, November 7, 1960, 8.
13. George Gallup, "Country Chairmen See Kennedy-Nixon Contest," *The Washington Post, Times Herald*, June 24, 1960, A2.
14. All of the quotes from this article came from "Editorial Opinion on Kennedy Victory," *New York Times*, June 15, 1960, 11, which compiled various quotes from various sources when talking about Kennedy's nomination.
15. "1960 Presidential Election Results," John F. Kennedy Presidential Library, www.jfklibrary.org/learn/about-jfk/life-of-john-f-kennedy/fast-facts-john-f-kennedy/1960-presidential-election-results (accessed March 3, 2019).
16. "Kennedy and the Cold War," John F. Kennedy Presidential Library, https://www.jfklibrary.org/learn/about-jfk/jfk-in-history/the-cold-war (accessed March 3, 2019).
17. George Gallup, "Kennedy's Rating High in Five Nations Abroad: Ratings in Major Cities," *The Washington Post, Times Herald*, January 21, 1961, A2.
18. "Changing Lives the World Over," Peace Corps, https://www.peacecorps.gov/about/ (accessed May 1, 2019).
19. *JFK Years of Lightning, Day of Drums*, Bruce Herschensohn, dir. (Embassy Picture Release, 1965), https://www.youtube.com/watch?v=E4EZB80rv5w (accessed March 3, 2019).
20. Douglass Cater, "How a President Helps Form Public Opinion," *New York Times*, February 26, 1961, SM12.
21. *JFK Years of Lightning, Day of Drums*.
22. Henry Bill, "A Bit of Color for Ayub Khan," *Los Angles Times*, July 9, 1961, E1.
23. "Kennedy Clan Goes Cruising: Attorney General Is Godfather for Niece," The

Washington Post, Times Herald, July 9, 1961, F2.

24. "Cuban Missile Crisis," John F. Kennedy Presidential Library, https://www.jfklibrary.org/learn/about-jfk/jfk-in-history/cuban-missile-crisis (accessed March 15, 2019).
25. Carl Greenberg, "Goldwater Fears Deal Over Cuba," *Los Angeles Times*, December 16, 1962, DA.
26. Gallup, "Presidential Approval Ratings – Gallup Historical Statistics and Trends," Gallup.com, https://news.gallup.com/poll/116677/presidential-approval-ratings-gallup-historical-statistics-trends.aspx (accessed April 1, 2019).
27. "Civil Rights Movement," JFK Library, https://www.jfklibrary.org/learn/about-jfk/jfk-in-history/civil-rights-movement (accessed April 14, 2019).
28. Louis Harris, "JFK Popularity Registers 59%," *Washington Post, Times Herald*, July 1, 1963, A1.
29. "John F. Kennedy Assassinated," History.com, November 24, 2009, https://www.history.com/this-day-in-history/john-f-kennedy-assassinated (accessed April 1, 2019).
30. Lyndon B. Johnson, "Address Before a Joint Session of the Congress, 27 November 1963," in *Public Papers of the Presidents of the United States: Lyndon B. Johnson, 1963–64*, vol. 1 (Washington, D.C.: Government Printing Office, 1964), 181–85.
31. Stewart Alsop, "Johnson Takes Over: The Untold Story," *The Saturday Evening Post*, February 15, 1964, 17–23.
32. Patrick Sloyan, "Kennedy Is Given 5-1 Edge to Be Rated Above Johnson," *Atlanta Constitution*, November 22, 1966, 1.
33. Dan Farrell, "John F. Kennedy Jr. Salutes His Father's Casket in Washington," photograph, 1963, Rare Historical Photos, October 14, 2017, https://rarehistoricalphotos.com/john-kennedy-salute-1963/ (accessed April 1, 2019).
34. Farrell, "John F. Kennedy Jr. Salutes His Father's Casket in Washington, 1963."
35. "Opinion of the Week: At Home and Abroad," *New York Times*, November 22, 1964, E9.
36. "JFK Restored Nation's Confidence, Attorney General Says in TV Appeal," *The Washington Post, Times Herald*, March 13, 1964, A13.
37. Louis Harris, "JFK Death Still Saddens 3 Out of 4; Mixture of Grief, Shame Prevails," *The Washington Post, Times Herald*, November 22, 1965, A2.

3. Red on the Horizon: The Cuban Missile Crisis and the 1963 Limited Test Ban Treaty

SETH HENDRICKSON

Dawn of a Nuclear Age

> *There were people crying out for help, calling after members of their family. I saw a schoolgirl with her eye hanging out of its socket. People looked like ghosts, bleeding and trying to walk before collapsing. Some had lost limbs. There were charred bodies everywhere, including in the river. I looked down and saw a man clutching a hole in his stomach, trying to stop his organs from spilling out. The smell of burning flesh was overpowering.*
>
> *There was so much smoke in the air that you could barely see 100 meters ahead, but what I did see convinced me that I had entered a living hell on earth.*
>
> – Sunao Tsuboi (survivor of the Hiroshima bombing)[1]

On August 6, 1945, the United States introduced the world to the destructive capabilities of nuclear weapons when it dropped an atomic bomb on Hiroshima, Japan. The bomb reduced thirteen square kilometers of the city to rubble, caused an estimated 135,000 Japanese casualties, and led to the scenes of horror described by Hiroshima survivor Sunao Tsuboi.[2] Three days later, the United States also bombed the city of Nagasaki, ushering in Japan's surrender and the end of World War II, as well as the beginning of an age of fear characterized by the rise of nuclear weapons and technology.

Almost two decades later, in his televised address on the final passage of the 1963 Limited Test Ban Treaty (LTBT), President Kennedy highlighted why the Soviet Union and United States had worked together towards arms control and passage of the LTBT. He foreshadowed a world devastated by nuclear war. He stated, "A full-scale nuclear war exchange lasting less than 60 minutes, could wipe out more than 300 million Americans, Europeans, and Russians." Crops would not be able to grow from the poisonous fallout, entire cities would be reduced to rubble, and global institutions and infrastructure would be devastated.[3] In just one hour the entire world would be flipped upside down and the survivors would inherit a living hell on Earth, just as Sunao Tsuboi had described.

Fear of nuclear proliferation, coupled with the ever-present threat of nuclear annihilation and health and environmental concerns of radioactive waste in the atmosphere, pushed the Eisenhower and Kennedy administrations towards negotiations with the Soviet Union on a test ban treaty.[4] Both the United States and Soviet Union feared nuclear war and wanted to slow the arms race. This mutual fear of nuclear war should have propelled both nations to quickly engage in more successful negotiations, but time and again, negotiations failed. For eighteen years the two states could not come to an agreement. Finally, in the wake of the Cuban Missile Crisis, which brought the world to the brink of nuclear war, the United States and Soviet Union finally came to an agreement to limit nuclear weapons testing.

Many historians reference the Cuban Missile Crisis as an event that marked a more cooperative approach to negotiations between the two states.[5] However, there is historical debate on what factors played a role in shifting the negotiations towards the passage of the 1963 Limited Test Ban Treaty. Many historians argue it was a combination of multiple factors, but each historian identifies a key factor. One school of thought argues that the Cuban Missile Crisis by itself wasn't enough to cause the shift but that it was caused by a number of global and political incidents. Other scholars argue that interest groups and public opinion had a profound impact on pushing negotiations. Still others insist that political heads like Kennedy and Khrushchev, and negotiators like Norman Cousins, were the reason the treaty moved along and was ultimately ratified.[6]

This chapter will examine how the negotiations for a nuclear test ban treaty changed following the Cuban Missile Crisis and why the United States and Soviet Union were able to overcome roadblocks that had plagued both the Eisenhower and Kennedy administrations. It argues that the two nations' ability to come to an agreement and ratify a treaty was the result of a combination of technological advancements, continued testing, as well as the driven and cooperative leadership of Kennedy and Khrushchev following the nuclear brinkmanship of October 1962. The Cuban Missile Crisis was a significant turning point in negotiations, as it reaffirmed the need and urgency for arms control and raised the possibility that the two superpowers could work together. Technological advancements allowed the United States to make concessions in negotiations regarding safeguard provisions. These factors, combined with a new capacity of knowledge on nuclear technology that made further testing unnecessary, meant that it was only a matter of time before the United States and Soviet Union passed a treaty. The combination of having, at the same time, both the will and the way to reach an agreement on arms control resulted in the passage of the 1963 Limited Test Ban Treaty.

The Road to the Limited Test Ban Treaty

In the wake of World War II, the United States and the Soviet Union emerged as world superpowers with very different ideologies: the former representing democracy and the latter representing communism. The difference between these respective ideologies caused tension between the two nations and led to the emergence of the Cold War. Worried about communist expansion under the Soviet Union, the United States adopted a policy of containment backed by military force and the threat of nuclear war.[7] This policy sparked an arms race between the two states as they competed over nuclear superiority.

As both the United States and Soviet Union continued to test and develop new and more powerful nuclear weapons, proponents of banning nuclear weapons and nuclear testing gained more support. Throughout his presidency, Dwight D. Eisenhower championed a nuclear test ban but was ultimately unable to reach an agreement with the Soviet Union. The two nations could not come to a consensus regarding what test environments would be banned, what safeguards would be implemented to ensure compliance, and who would make up the overarching control organization. When these negotiations would reach an impasse, the two nations would often resume nuclear testing, which further complicated and delayed a possible weapons testing ban.

When President John F. Kennedy came into office, he met similar roadblocks in his negotiations for a nuclear test ban treaty with the Soviet Union as his predecessor had.[8] From October 16 to October 28 of 1962, the threat of nuclear war seemed close to becoming a reality as the United States discovered Soviet nuclear missile sites being built in Cuba. To combat this national security threat, the United States established a naval blockade around Cuba.[9] In October 1962, the two states found themselves in a standoff and on the brink of nuclear annihilation. During this event, known as the Cuban Missile Crisis, both President Kennedy and Soviet Premier Nikita Khrushchev recognized how destructive nuclear war would be and worked together to end the crisis. Within a year of the crisis, the United States and Soviet Union finally overcame the old barriers in negotiations and came to an agreement on the Limited Test Ban Treaty.

National Security, Fear, and Skepticism

Throughout the Cold War, national security and the fear of nuclear destruction weighed heavily on the minds of the American public. The Cuban Missile Crisis was the epitome of a nuclear national security threat, as it was the first time Soviet nuclear weapons directly threatened the United States. Located on an island just 103 miles off the coast of Florida, a nuclear missile launched from Cuba could target and wipe out just about any major city in the United States.[10] Although the Soviets ultimately removed their missiles from Cuba, the American people were still frightened and fearful of a nuclear war in the crisis's aftermath. How could Americans trust the Soviets after they had just tried to secretly set up missile sites in Cuba? How could Americans trust the Soviets to take an arms control treaty seriously? These questions are critical to understanding why it took so long to establish a nuclear test ban treaty. This section will examine the role fear and skepticism played in negotiations towards the Limited Test Ban Treaty. It will also look at the legacy of the 1963 LTBT's limited accomplishments in reducing the United States' fear or slowing the arms race.

Mistrust between the Soviet Union and United States often prolonged the negotiations to reach a test ban treaty. Both nations were unwilling to accept the other's proposals since the two nations could not agree on what safeguards would be implemented. The major arguing point that stalled negotiations was related to on-site inspections of unidentified earth tremors that may have been caused by underground nuclear tests. In January 1960, the Soviets made a proposal that would allow three inspections per year, but only if there was scientific evidence that warranted an inspection. The United States immediately rejected this proposal on the grounds that such a limited number of inspections would not be realistic in determining whether such incidents were caused by natural tremors or man-induced underground testing.[11] In negotiations, the Soviet Union was concerned that the United States and its allies would preside over the inspection teams and other safeguard organizations in order to gather reconnaissance on Soviet sites, weapon stockpiles, and test data.[12] The Soviets did not trust the West and wanted to retain control of operations in their own territory. As a result, they remained unyielding on negotiations regarding inspection limits and treaty safeguards. The United States, however, was skeptical of whether or not the Soviet Union would try to cheat a test ban treaty. With a limited number of allowed inspections, the US felt it could not adequately ensure Soviet compliance with a proposed treaty. Since the United States and Soviet Union both felt that they could not trust each other, the two nations were unable to agree on what safeguards would be implemented in a test ban treaty, and thus further stalled negotiations.

When negotiations between the United States and Soviet Union stalled, the resumption of nuclear weapons testing created tension and feelings of fear between the two nations and, in the process, pushed the possibility of passing a test ban treaty further out of reach. In October 1961, in the midst of negotiations towards a peace treaty with East Germany, Soviet Premier Khrushchev announced that the USSR would conduct a series of nuclear weapons tests, including a fifty-megaton test on October 30. Khrushchev's announcement sparked a wave of fear in the United States. The Cuban Missile Crisis made things even worse. In his 1965 article "Halloween, the 50-Megaton Bomb, and the Cuban Crisis," Pierre Lacombe analyzes how the American press reacted to the announcement of the tests and mega-bomb using symbolic imagery and myths of Halloween and other ancient traditions that celebrate ancestors, spirits, the dead, and the coming of winter. Articles such as "Who's Afraid of Witches" compared Khrushchev's role to that of a witch on Halloween.[13] Lacombe similarly compared the fear of winter and the long night that ancestors feared to the persistent anxiety and fear that the American population had of a nuclear winter.[14] In his paper Lacombe asked, "Are not we closer than they were to the final darkness in which the latest atomic discoveries, the race of the super-bomb and the feverish build-up of missiles, can suddenly engulf us all?"[15] Every additional nuclear weapon created by the US or USSR during the arms race increased the possible destruction that would be caused if a nuclear war were to break out. The resumed testing that resulted from continuous failure to reach an agreement on an arms treaty created a sense of fear that nuclear war was still a very real possibility and that arms treaty negotiations would not succeed.

After the Cuban Missile Crisis, both the United States and Soviet Union realized the need for a treaty that might slow the arms race. On July 26, 1963, President Kennedy gave a televised address to the nation on the conclusion of negotiations and passage of the LTBT. In his speech, Kennedy hailed the treaty as a "victory for mankind," because it opened the political door to more talks on comprehensive negotiations and the prevention of nuclear proliferation.[16] At the same time, Kennedy made it clear that the treaty was a *limited* one. On-site inspections and other safeguard provisions that the US and USSR had long argued over never made it into the 1963 LTBT. The treaty required "no control posts, no on-site inspections and no international body."[17] The treaty also did little towards preventing nuclear war. As Kennedy stated, "It will not reduce nuclear stockpiles; it will not halt the production of nuclear weapons; [and] it will not restrict their use in time of war."[18] Following the treaty's ratification, the arms race continued and weapon stockpiles increased at an even faster rate than before.[19] Even though the LTBT did little to slow the arms race or ease fear and tension between the United States and Soviet Union, the successful passage of the 1963 Limited Test Ban Treaty marked a landmark agreement between the US and the USSR.

The United States and Soviet Union knew that the LTBT would be restricted in its provisions, which caused the two nations to work together and provide a way to protect and ensure their national security from threats posed by other states. The expansion of the French and Chinese nuclear programs, as examples, persisted as a possible international threat. In response, the 1963 LTBT included a provision which allowed any treaty-signing nation to remove itself if it felt that non-treaty parties, such as France and China, were testing nuclear weapons to an extent that threatened the treaty-signing nation's national security.[20] This provision allowed both the United States and Soviet Union the ability to protect its national security interests from possible international threats while still adhering to the treaty.

As the LTBT was under negotiation, there was a sense of skepticism about whether or not the Soviet Union could be trusted to honor the treaty. However, in the years following the passage of the LTBT, Americans agreed that it was generally a good idea to have signed the treaty. In March 1963, the Gallup Organization asked US adults whether or not they thought the USSR would live up to its agreement. Only 19% of the population surveyed said yes; 65% said no.[21] A year after the treaty had passed, in 1964, Louis Harris & Associates conducted its own poll asking a sample of US adults whether or not they favored the passage of the LTBT: 83% of those polled favored the treaty and 17% opposed.[22] They conducted the same poll again in 1966, with similar results: 75% favored the treaty, 8% thought it was a bad idea, and 17% were unsure.[23] There may have been a general consensus that the American public approved of the treaty, but the treaty still did little to assuage its concerns.

On January 15, 1965, the headline of a 1965 *Chicago Tribune* article, "Russians Deny Violation of A-Test Treaty," justified the long-standing skepticism the United States held with regards to whether it could trust the Soviet Union. An underground Soviet nuclear test reportedly "spread radioactivity beyond the borders of the Soviet Union."[24] This action violated article 1, section b, of the LTBT, which states:

> Each of the Parties to this Treaty undertakes to prohibit, to prevent, and not to carry out any nuclear weapon test explosion, or any other nuclear explosion, at any place under its jurisdiction or control in any other environment if such explosion causes radioactive debris to be present outside the territorial limits of the State under whose jurisdiction or control such explosion is conducted.[25]

The Soviet defense of this incident was that "the nuclear explosion was carried out deep underground ... and that some radioactive debris leaked into the atmosphere."[26] But to say that nuclear fallout found in the atmosphere over Japan from a Soviet nuclear test was just "an accident" seems to make light of a serious issue. The US and USSR had been pushing to limit and control nuclear tests for years, and this response belittled all the efforts made to pass the LTBT. The United States eventually dropped the issue, and the Soviets better controlled subsequent testing. But what reassurance did the American population have that the Soviets would not violate the treaty again? Despite the passage of LTBT, the United States was still fearful and skeptical of whether or not the Soviet Union could be trusted to honor it.

Negotiations towards the LTBT of 1963 were often delayed as a result of mutual distrust between the Soviet Union and the United States. The US was often skeptical of the Soviets as negotiations regarding safeguards often remained at an impasse. The USSR did not want Western-dominated inspection teams to check and spy on Soviet sites. Resumed testing during these stalemates also complicated negotiations as the United States wanted to ensure its nuclear superiority over the USSR, and often further delayed negotiations. Finally, when the US and USSR agreed on the LTBT of 1963, its severely limited provisions resulted in continued feelings of skepticism and fear.

How Technology Changed the LTBT Negotiations

The Soviets were not solely to blame for the stalemates in negotiations towards a test ban treaty. Fear and mistrust of the Soviet Union pushed the United States to continue to develop new technology so that it could better verify if the Soviet Union had conducted nuclear tests without the need for on-site inspections. At the same time, the United States also resumed its own nuclear testing to ensure its nuclear superiority over the Soviet Union. Writer David Inglis argued, in the January edition of the 1963 *Bulletin of the Atomic Scientists*, that the American policy of maintaining a distinct nuclear superiority over the USSR was "a policy incompatible with the pursuit of arms control and disarmament."[27] This section examines how continued testing and improvements in equipment and technology allowed the Kennedy administration to shift its negotiating position and succeed in passing a test ban treaty. Kennedy succeeded where Eisenhower failed because continued testing and innovations in technology made further nuclear tests in the atmosphere and underwater inessential. This allowed the United States to feel that it could adequately monitor and police Soviet underground testing without treaty safeguards.

As the United States and Soviet Union began to reach a capacity of knowledge on nuclear testing, the new information each nation gained from continued atmospheric, space, and underwater nuclear testing stopped being worth the money or energy invested in continuing the tests. While there was still more to learn from continued atmospheric weapons testing, concerns about the destructive nature of the tests on the environment, coupled with health concerns about nuclear fallout in the atmosphere, drowned out advocates for further testing. In 1960, during a test moratorium, the US made a proposal for joint testing, in which the nuclear weapon states would conduct nuclear tests together and share their findings and data.[28] This proposal would have lowered the overall number of nuclear tests being conducted while at the same time allowing further testing and gathering of information. However, it would rely heavily on trust and cooperation between the two states. This cooperation was difficult to achieve. Although such an agreement would have been beneficial to both the United States and the Soviet Union, the Soviets were still working to catch up to the United States. Mutual feelings of distrust and skepticism between the two nations also made it unlikely that the two nations would agree. Not surprisingly, the Soviets rejected this proposal on the basis that it was a resumption of weapons development by the United States. This decision nullified the moratorium and allowed the USSR to resume and pursue its own tests. By 1962, with continued testing, the Soviets caught up with the United States in terms of understanding the results from atmospheric and underwater nuclear tests. As both nations reached a capacity of knowledge, further testing in the atmosphere, space, and underwater became unnecessary.

Besides safeguards, the United States and Soviet Union also argued about whether or not underground testing would be allowed in a test ban treaty. At the beginning of test ban negotiations, the United States was a proponent for continuing to allow underground testing, but ongoing testing allowed the United States to shift its position. By July 1962, the United States began to reach its capacity of information on underground tests. Secretary of Defense Robert McNamara wrote to President Kennedy informing him that a test ban treaty would be in the United States' favor. In his memo, McNamara argued that "further testing would enable both sides to make only modest increases ... since both sides [were] already close to their limits."[29] However, he also stated that continued testing could grant the United States more knowledge about how nuclear explosions affected communication devices, radar, and anti-missile systems. But information of that nature was difficult to predict. McNamara also asserted that continued testing would not significantly affect the American-Soviet military balance, whereas a ban would secure the American advantage and slow further developments made by other nuclear weapon states. This development allowed the United States to return to negotiations with its nuclear superiority and the ability to agree on banning underground testing in addition to the other environments.

The change in the United States' position on the key roadblocks of safeguards and testing environments allowed the US and USSR to come to an agreement on a test ban treaty. Since the United States and the Soviet Union had each achieved an understanding of nuclear knowledge that rendered further testing unnecessary, it is no surprise that the two states were able to come to an agreement to ban further tests in those environments. However, as the two states were still gathering data from underground tests, they allowed underground testing to persist. As a result, the 1963 LTBT only specifically banned tests in "the atmosphere; beyond its limits, including outer space; or under water, including territorial waters or high seas."[30] Advances in reconnaissance technology also allowed the US to shift its stance on safeguard provisions, since the US felt that it could adequately monitor the USSR through satellites and detection stations, all without the need of on-site inspections and inspection teams. Continued testing and technological advancements thus allowed both the United States and Soviet Union to overcome old roadblocks and agree on a test ban treaty.

Kennedy's advisors pushed for the United States to work towards a non-proliferation treaty along with a test ban treaty. Nuclear proliferation, or the spread of nuclear weapons to other nations, was a major concern during the arms race, as it had the potential to cause a major shift in the global balance of powers. The United States, Soviet Union, and the United Kingdom were the three major nuclear weapon states working towards a test ban treaty. France and Communist China were close to becoming nuclear weapon states as well, and it was unlikely that either of those two nations would initially sign a test ban treaty that would slow their progress towards becoming nuclear weapon states. The Arms Control and Disarmament Agency advised Kennedy that even if China and/or France did not sign the LTBT, the treaty would still be in favor of US and Soviet interests.[31] In addition, the agency argued that if a test ban passed, the US could pressure France and the USSR could pressure China to restrict their respective nuclear programs and prevent further proliferation. Following the ratification of the LTBT, the US and USSR continued to work together on treaties for a more comprehensive test ban against nuclear proliferation and for disarmament, leading to the 1968 passage of the Nuclear Non-Proliferation Treaty.

President Kennedy was able to succeed in passing a test ban treaty where his predecessor failed as a result of continued testing and technological advancements. During the Eisenhower Administration, the United States was still gathering new information and data from nuclear tests. There was also no safeguard against Soviet testing, as the two states could not come to an agreement on on-site inspections. Comparatively, during the Kennedy administration, the United States reached a capacity of knowledge that made further testing unnecessary, while the improvement of reconnaissance technologies allowed the United States to monitor the Soviet Union without on-site inspections. In both administrations, the United States had a technological and militaristic superiority over the Soviet Union, but it was the further advances in technology and continued testing that paved the way for the United States and the Soviet Union to overcome obstacles that had long prevented a mutual agreement.

Peaceful Coexistence During the Cold War

In his 1961 farewell address, Eisenhower noted that he was leaving the presidency with a "definite sense of disappointment" around his inability to pass a test ban treaty.[32] Although he failed, Eisenhower made it clear that the objective to reach "disarmament, with mutual honor and confidence, [was] a continuing imperative" and that, as a nation, "we must learn how to compose difference, not with arms, but with intellect and decent purpose."[33] Following the Cuban Missile Crisis, President Kennedy worked together with Soviet Premier Khrushchev; both leaders realized the importance and necessity of slowing the arms race and preventing nuclear war.[34] Together Kennedy and Khrushchev were able to make small, but impactful, strides towards détente, peaceful coexistence, and improved relations through their actions and rhetoric and were ultimately able to ratify a test ban treaty.

In a secret negotiation that helped resolve the Cuban Missile Crisis, Khrushchev and Kennedy took the first important step towards détente and disarmament. As part of the negotiated agreement, the Soviets agreed to remove missiles from Cuba if the United States agreed not to invade Cuba and to remove US missiles located in countries neighboring the USSR, such as Turkey.[35] As the two nations resumed negotiations towards a test ban treaty, Soviet delegate Valerian A. Zorin stated that the events in Cuba demonstrated "the good faith of the Soviet Union in trying to avert war" and that the Soviet Union was a peace-loving state.[36] This statement came under criticism from US delegate Arthur H. Dean, who questioned how a state could be peace-loving "for having agreed to remove the very weapons it had put there."[37] This criticism, however, was hypocritical, as the US had secretly put its own missiles in Turkey, aimed at the Soviet Union, in order to protect US interests and national security. The removal of missiles by both the United States and Soviet Union was thus a first step towards détente.

The second step in opening negotiations and moving towards détente and the prevention of nuclear war was the establishment of the Direct Communications Link (DCL), commonly known as the "hotline" or "red telephone." This DCL between the Pentagon and the Kremlin allowed for clearer and faster communication between the two states and their leaders. The link became operational in June 1963, but Kennedy and Khrushchev never communicated through it since the first formal communication sent was news of Kennedy's assassination.[38] The establishment of the Direct Communications Link following the Cuban Missile Crisis, however, made it possible for the two nations to work together, with faster and clearer communication, in order to resolve future crises.

The possibility of passing a test ban treaty proved more favorable as the leaders of the United States and Soviet Union made a shift towards détente in their rhetoric as well as their actions. In his speech "A Strategy of Peace," President Kennedy addressed a plan to slow and limit the arms race he believed was one of the greatest hazards of the time.[39] To reach his goal of complete disarmament of nuclear weapons, Kennedy announced that he would soon begin working with Khrushchev towards an "early agreement on a comprehensive test ban treaty." As a show of good faith, Kennedy also declared that the United States would not resume nuclear tests in the atmosphere unless other states did. Perhaps the most peaceful overture to the Soviet Union was in his closing remarks:

> The United States, as the world knows, will never start a war. We do not want a war. We do not now expect a war. ... We shall be prepared if others wish it. We shall be alert to try to stop it. But we shall also do our part to build a world of peace where the weak are safe and the strong are just.[40]

A CIA information report on the Soviet response to the president's speech revealed that the Soviets believed the speech created a positive atmosphere for further cooperation and negotiations, as the speech "reflected a broad progressive approach towards solving current problems."[41] The report outlined how the speech eased Soviet doubts of US sincerity towards a test ban treaty. Following the pro-US-Soviet rhetoric of the speech, the possibility of the United States and Soviet Union agreeing on a test ban treaty seemed very favorable.

The rhetoric employed by Khrushchev held that peaceful coexistence between the US and USSR, and a test ban treaty, was possible despite opposition. Khrushchev's goals of a test ban treaty and peaceful coexistence came under hypocritical criticism from Soviet military leaders as well as communist Chinese leaders. The Chinese were working to develop their own nuclear weapons while maintaining the stance that there should be a ban on their use, manufacturing, stockpiling, and testing. The Chinese criticized Khrushchev and argued that "socialist countries have no need for nuclear weapons."[42] However, as the Soviets were in the middle of an arms race and had recently reached the brink of nuclear war, the Soviet premier took a personal interest in the test ban debates. Khrushchev's actions and rhetoric directly reflect the positive atmosphere for further cooperation and negotiations of a test ban previously mentioned in the CIA report.

On July 14, 1963, reflecting the shared desire to reach détente, Khrushchev met with American and British representatives in the Kremlin to re-open test ban talks between the three nuclear powers. During these talks, Kennedy instructed the US delegate to attempt to reach a comprehensive test ban, but if a comprehensive ban was not possible, he would still consider a limited test ban a step in the right direction. A limited test ban would open up the door to later negotiations and discussions towards a comprehensive ban.[43] The threat of nuclear war was still a possibility, but improved American-Soviet relations produced a more relaxed international climate.[44] This new international climate allowed the United States and Soviet Union to build on the success of a limited or comprehensive test ban.

Mutual respect, similar goals, and improved relations between President Kennedy and Premier Khrushchev after the Cuban Missile Crisis paved the way for improved relations between the United States and the Soviet Union. As both leaders took actions towards détente and improved communication to prevent future crises between the two nations, the possibility of passing a nuclear test ban treaty became more likely. Both leaders also made a shift in rhetoric as they exemplified a strong will to work towards a treaty regardless of foreign influence. Together, building off of the advancements in technology and continued testing, Kennedy and Khrushchev worked together to pass a test ban treaty and improve relations between their two nations.

Legacy of the Limited Test Ban Treaty

President Kennedy's cooperation and openness may have been key components in furthering negotiations with Khrushchev, but Kennedy needed to convince the Senate that it was in the best interest of the United States to ratify the LTBT. In an attempt to convince the Senate to ratify the treaty, Kennedy wrote a special message outlining why the treaty was beneficial. Kennedy's major arguments to the Senate for passing the treaty were that it would curb both the arms race and pollution of the atmosphere; ensure US nuclear superiority; promise stability, as the treaty could not be amended without US consent; and, most importantly, lead to further control measures and treaties.[45] For eighteen years the United States had made an effort to impose limitations on nuclear testing and slow the arms race, and this was the first successful treaty negotiated with the Soviet Union. Acting in the United States' best interests and to preserve the nation's global status, the US Senate ratified the Limited Test Ban Treaty on October 10, 1963.

The United States' and Soviet Union's desire to seek an agreement on a treaty that would limit nuclear weapons testing in the middle of an arms race seemed like an improbable goal. This objective put the two nations in a complicated situation. For a long time, the US and USSR could not agree on what safeguards should be implemented to monitor compliance with the treaty, as well as if underground testing should be banned. As a result of fear and mistrust, the two states were often inconclusive in negotiations. For eighteen years the two states struggled to come to an agreement.

The Cuban Missile Crisis was a significant turning point in American-Soviet negotiations, as it reaffirmed the need and urgency for arms control, raised the possibility that the two superpowers could work together, and proved that positive East-West relations were possible. During the Eisenhower administration, the two states would often resume testing, which further prolonged and disrupted the negotiation process. During the Kennedy administration, the mutual respect that developed between Kennedy and Khrushchev because of the crisis, coupled with their leadership roles and commitment to not resume testing, allowed the US and USSR to be more conclusive in negotiations.

While the Cuban Missile Crisis may have expedited the passage of an arms treaty, the passage of such a treaty was bound to happen eventually. The two nations, in fact, would not have been able to come to an agreement if not for the continuous testing and technological advances made prior to the Cuban Missile Crisis. Old roadblocks such as skepticism, safeguards, and environmental provisions were no longer as hotly debated. Years of continued testing had allowed both states to reach a capacity of knowledge that made further testing in environments such as in the atmosphere and underwater unnecessary. Advances in reconnaissance technology also allowed the United States to have a sense of security since it thought it could now adequately monitor and police nuclear testing through satellites and detection stations. Even if Kennedy had failed to come to an agreement with the Soviet Union, these factors and developments made it easier for the United States and Soviet Union to work together at the negotiation table, and it was only a matter of time before a test ban treaty would have been established.

In 1963, the United States and Soviet Union passed the Limited Test Ban Treaty of 1963 and together accomplished an improbable goal. The treaty was very limited in its provisions and failed to accomplish many of the secondary objectives the US hoped it would. The arms race continued throughout the Cold War, weapon stockpiles grew, more countries developed nuclear weapons, and the fear of nuclear annihilation lingered. Nevertheless, the treaty accomplished its major objectives: it banned nuclear tests in the atmosphere, underwater, and in space; it opened up talks on future arms treaties and negotiations; and by the end of the Cold War it helped the world avoid the creation of a "living hell on earth"[46] from nuclear war.

Notes

1. Tsuboi Sunao quoted in Justin McCurry, "The Man Who Survived Hiroshima: 'I Had Entered a Living Hell on Earth,'" *The Guardian*, August 4, 2015.
2. "Total Casualties," The Atomic Bombings of Hiroshima and Nagasaki, http://www.atomicarchive.com/Docs/MED/med_chp10.shtml (accessed March 3, 2019).
3. John F. Kennedy, "Radio and Television Address to the Nation on Nuclear Test Ban Treaty," speech, Washington, DC, July 26, 1963, John F. Kennedy Presidential Library and Museum, https://www.jfklibrary.org/asset-viewer/archives/JFKPOF/046/JFKPOF-046-008 (accessed March 4, 2019).
4. For more information regarding test ban negotiations during the Eisenhower and Kennedy Administrations, refer to: Lisa A. Baglione, *To Agree or Not to Agree: Leadership, Bargaining, and Arms Control* (Ann Arbor: University of Michigan Press, 1999); Thanos P. Dokos, *Negotiations for a CTBT 1958-1994: Analysis and Evaluation of American Policy* (Lanham, MD: University Press of America, 1995); Benjamin P. Greene, *Eisenhower, Science Advice, and the Nuclear Test-Ban Debate, 1945-1963*, Stanford Nuclear Age Series (Stanford: Stanford University Press, 2007); and James H. Lebovic, *Flawed Logics: Strategic Nuclear Arms Control from Truman to Obama* (Baltimore: Johns Hopkins University Press, 2013).
5. For general information on the Cuban Missile Crisis, see: Robert F. Kennedy, Harold Macmillan, and Sam Sloan, *Thirteen Days: A Memoir of the Cuban Missile Crisis* (Ishi Press International, 2017); and Michelle Getchell, *The Cuban Missile Crisis and the Cold War: A Short History with Documents* (Indianapolis: Hackett Publishing Company, 2018).
6. For arguments regarding interest groups and public opinion as major factors in negotiations: James E. Goodby, "The Limited Test Ban Negotiations, 1954-63: How a Negotiator Viewed the Proceedings," *International Negotiation* 10, no. 3 (2005): 381-404, https://doi.org/10.1163/157180605776087507; and James Cameron, *The Double Game: The Demise of America's First Missile Defense System and the Rise of Strategic Arms Limitation* (New York: Oxford University Press, 2018). For arguments referring to political leaders and negotiators: Baglione, *To Agree or Not to Agree* and Allen Pietrobon, "The Role of Norman Cousins and Track II Diplomacy in the Breakthrough to the 1963 Limited Test Ban Treaty," *Journal of Cold War Studies* 18, no. 1 (Winter 2016): 60-79, https://doi.org/10.1162/JCWS_a_00619 (accessed March 2, 2019).
7. More on American policy during the Cold War reference Baglione, *To Agree or Not to Agree*.
8. For reference on negotiations during the Eisenhower and Kennedy Administra-

tions: Dokos, *Negotiations for a CTBT 1958-1994*; and Greene, *Eisenhower, Science Advice, and the Nuclear Test-Ban Debate*.
9. For US handling of the CMC: Getchell, *The Cuban Missile Crisis*; and Kennedy et al., *Thirteen Days*.
10. Diana Nyad, "Cuba: So Close You Could Almost Swim There," *HuffPost*, December 7, 2017.
11. "Soviet Compromise Bid on Test Ban is Rejected," *The Washington Post*, January 14, 1960, Times Herald (1959–1973), A10.
12. Dokos, *Negotiations For a CTBT 1958–1994*, 9.
13. Pierre Lacombe, "Halloween, the 50-Megaton Bomb, and the Cuban Crisis," *Journal of Analytical Psychology* 10, no. 1 (1965): 97.
14. Lacombe, "Halloween, the 50-Megaton Bomb, and the Cuban Crisis."
15. Lacombe, "Halloween, the 50-Megaton Bomb, and the Cuban Crisis," 107.
16. John F. Kennedy, radio and television address to the nation on nuclear test ban treaty, July 26, 1963.
17. John F. Kennedy, address on nuclear test ban treaty, July 26, 1963.
18. John F. Kennedy, address on nuclear test ban treaty, July 26, 1963.
19. Dokos, *Negotiations for a CTBT 1958–1994*, 2, 33, 98.
20. Arms Control and Disarmament Agency, "Relationship of Nuclear Test Ban to Problem of Proliferation of Nuclear Weapons," February 13, 1963, in William Burr and Hector L. Montford, eds., "The Making of the Limited Test Ban Treaty, 1958–1963," August 8, 2003, https://nsarchive2.gwu.edu/NSAEBB/NSAEBB94/index2.htm (accessed April 4, 2019).
21. Gallup Organization. Gallup Poll (AIPO), Mar, 1963 [survey question], US GALLUP.63-669.R020. Gallup Organization [producer], Cornell University, Ithaca, NY: Roper Center for Public Opinion Research, iPOLL [distributor], https://bit.ly/2UGrhN8 (accessed April 16, 2019).
22. Louis Harris & Associates. Harris Survey, Dec, 1964 [survey question], US HARRIS.122864.R3. Louis Harris & Associates [producer], Cornell University, Ithaca, NY: Roper Center for Public Opinion Research, iPOLL [distributor], https://bit.ly/2UGrlwm (accessed April 16, 2019).
23. Louis Harris & Associates. Harris Survey, Oct, 1966 [survey question], US HARRIS.101666.R2. Louis Harris & Associates [producer], Cornell University, Ithaca, NY: Roper Center for Public Opinion Research, iPOLL [distributor], https://bit.ly/2Pg5qWZ (accessed April 16, 2019).
24. Donald Philip, "Russians Deny Violation of A-test Treaty," *Chicago Tribune*, January 26, 1965, A11.
25. "Treaty Banning Nuclear Weapon Tests in the Atmosphere, in Outer Space and Under Water," August 5, 1963, US Department of State, https://www.state.gov/t/isn/4797.htm (accessed April 16, 2019).
26. Philip, "Russians Deny Violation of A-test Treaty."
27. David R. Inglis, "Disarmament after Cuba," *Bulletin of the Atomic Scientists* 19, no. 1 (January 1963): 18, http://login.ezproxy.lib.vt.edu/login?url=http://search.ebscohost.com/login.aspx?direct=true&db=edb&AN=21410301&site=eds-live&scope=site (accessed April 12, 2019).
28. Central Intelligence Agency, Office of Current Intelligence, *Current Intelligence Weekly Summary*, August 24, 1960, excerpt of "The Nuclear Test Ban Talks," in William Burr and Hector L. Montford, eds., "The Making of the Limited Test Ban

Treaty, 1958-1963," August 8, 2003, https://nsarchive2.gwu.edu/NSAEBB/NSAEBB94/index2.htm (accessed April 4, 2019).

29. Memorandum from Secretary of Defense McNamara to President Kennedy, "US-USSR Military Balance With or Without a Test Ban," circa July 1962, in William Burr and Hector L. Montford, eds., "The Making of the Limited Test Ban Treaty, 1958-1963," August 8, 2003, https://nsarchive2.gwu.edu/NSAEBB/NSAEBB94/index2.htm (accessed April 4, 2019).

30. "Treaty Banning Nuclear Weapon Tests," US Department of State.

31. Arms Control and Disarmament Agency, "Relationship of Nuclear Test Ban to Problem of Proliferation of Nuclear Weapons," February 13, 1963, in William Burr and Hector L. Montford, eds., "The Making of the Limited Test Ban Treaty, 1958-1963," August 8, 2003, https://nsarchive2.gwu.edu/NSAEBB/NSAEBB94/index2.htm (accessed April 4, 2019).

32. Dwight D. Eisenhower, "Farewell Radio and Television Address to the American People," speech, Washington, DC, January 17, 1961, Eisenhower Archives, https://www.eisenhowerlibrary.gov/sites/default/files/file/farewell_address.pdf (accessed March 3, 2019).

33. Eisenhower, "Farewell Address."

34. For general information on the Cuban Missile Crisis: Kennedy et al., *Thirteen Days*.

35. "Khrushchev on the Need for Relaxation of Tensions, 30 October 1962," in Jussi M. Hanhimäki and Odd Arne Westad, eds., *The Cold War: A History in Documents and EyeWitness Accounts* (Oxford: Oxford University Press, 2013), 488-90.

36. "Soviet Compromise Bid," A10.

37. "Soviet Compromise Bid," A10.

38. Crypto Museum, "Washington-Moscow Hotline," September 3, 2018, https://www.cryptomuseum.com/crypto/hotline/index.htm#ref (accessed March 6, 2019).

39. Commencement Address by President John F. Kennedy at American University in Washington, DC, June 10, 1963, in William Burr and Hector L. Montford, eds., "The Making of the Limited Test Ban Treaty, 1958-1963," August 8, 2003, https://nsarchive2.gwu.edu/NSAEBB/NSAEBB94/index2.htm (accessed March 3, 2019).

40. Kennedy, "Commencement Address."

41. CIA Information Report, "Soviet Reaction to June 10 Speech of President Kennedy," June 11, 1963, in William Burr and Hector L. Montford, eds., "The Making of the Limited Test Ban Treaty, 1958-1963," August 8, 2003, https://nsarchive2.gwu.edu/NSAEBB/NSAEBB94/index2.htm (accessed March 3, 2019).

42. "Excerpts from Khrushchev's Speech and Peking's Attack on Test-Ban Efforts," *New York Times*, July 20, 1963, 2.

43. Mark Frankland, "K to Open Test-Ban Talks Today," *The Washington Post*, July 15, 1963, A1.

44. Seymore Topping, "Detente? Moscow Intentions Are Veiled," *New York Times*, July 14, 1963, 113.

45. John F. Kennedy, "Message Sent to Senate by Kennedy on A-Test Ban," *The Washington Post*, August 9, 1963, Times Herald (1959-1973), A12.

46. McCurry, "The Man Who Survived Hiroshima."

4. Atlanta's Model Cities Program: A Boondoggle, Farce, and Ultimate Failure

BRIANNA SCLAFANI

> The whole poverty program is a monster devised to pay a "freight charge" to the leeches who deliver the "poor" vote. It was conceived in infamy – not humanity.
>
> – Mack Moore, Letter to the Editor, October 1970[1]

The disdain citizens felt towards President Lyndon Johnson's War on Poverty can be no better described than by this quote from Atlanta economist, activist, and citizen Mack A. Moore. In his series of letters to the editor of the *Atlanta Constitution*, Moore expressed the sentiments of African Americans in his community who felt they were being cheated out of the benefits of Johnson's War on Poverty, particularly when it came to housing. The Model Cities Program, designed almost solely by Johnson, was intended to fix the urban housing crisis of the 1960s. From Moore's perspective, however, the Model Cities Program that Atlanta officials desperately tried to implement was wasteful and pointless, even if it gave the appearance of having value. The program was, in his words, a "boondoggle."[2]

While LBJ saw the War on Poverty as his political masterpiece, it failed in many ways. The Johnson administration declared an unconditional War on Poverty in January of 1964 and called upon all of America to help with the fight. Officials outlined a multifaceted approach to the project, which was designed to help "that one fifth of all American families with incomes too small to even meet basic needs."[3] The administration wanted to improve the quality of American life and increase economic opportunities for the nation's poorest citizens. Some programs were designed to improve opportunities available to impoverished Americans while others worked to create an economic safety net for the poor.[4] Some well-known initiatives included the Food Stamp Act of 1964 and the Social Security Act of 1965, as well as the Demonstration Cities and Metropolitan Development Act of 1966, which introduced the Model Cities Program.

The Model Cities Program (MCP) aimed to combat housing discrimination and inadequate housing in urban areas. It was designed to weave together various aspects of community development.[5] With this new program, officials hoped that local community and federal partnerships could be established in order to treat all urban problems collectively.[6] The term *model cities* came from the idea that this new federal and local partnership would bypass traditional agency boundaries.[7] The idea was that Model Cities would ensure cooperation at all levels of government and planning. One of the cities that took advantage of this program was Atlanta.

Most historical discussions of the War on Poverty make broad generalizations about the success or failure of antipoverty initiatives enacted in the 1960s. Some explore specific aspects of LBJ's war. Scholars like Annelise Orleck have examined the implications of race pertaining to welfare rights and grassroots activism.[8] Others, such as author Kenneth Heineman, identify the hostility of white southerners as a key reason for the War on Poverty's limited success.[9] Through this lens, these writers offer insight about whether specific programs, attitudes, or policy strategies helped or hindered the war.

This chapter explores the failure of the Atlanta Model Cities Program. Using material from local newspapers as its primary guide, this chapter addresses how the Model Cities Program perpetuated racial and economic segregation, how the program affected power dynamics between officials and citizens, and how members of both the black and white communities viewed the program. The progressive national agenda of the Model Cities Program failed to be implemented in Atlanta. Biased Atlanta officials created discriminatory initiatives and used the program to maintain and secure their political power. These officials alienated Atlanta residents, which led to a lack of support for the program. The Model Cities Program was just as Moore described, a monster.

The Origins of the War on Poverty and Atlanta's Model Cities Program

The War on Poverty was a federal initiative designed to relieve, cure, and above all else prevent poverty.[10] LBJ took this task on as a project under the mantle of his Great Society. Johnson was dedicated to domestic issues, and historians cite the New Deal as his inspiration for the War on Poverty. But while the New Deal was launched during a period of high unemployment and the economic crisis of the Great Depression, the War on Poverty was launched during a period of relative prosperity.[11] This "war" initiated a new era of direct federal involvement in schools, labor markets, and neighborhoods. Johnson believed that the "federal government could and should provide poor Americans the resources they needed."[12]

Federal legislators and agencies created specific programs to oversee particular aspects of this initiative. This was certainly true for the Model Cities Program. The Demonstration Cities and Metropolitan Development Act of 1966 laid out the goals for the Model Cities Program. Its diverse aims included "expand[ed] housing, job, and income opportunities; [enhanced] recreational and cultural opportunities; better access between houses and jobs; and generally [improved] living conditions."[13] The Department of Housing and Urban Development (HUD), under the supervision of Secretary Robert Weaver, was given responsibility over the funds for the Model Cities Program. This was one of the many programs outlined by LBJ's War on Poverty.

Atlanta was one of a limited number of cities that took advantage of the Model Cities Program. Other major cities seemed uninterested. The Washington Bureau of the *Atlanta Constitution* wrote that "only 190 urban communities – including six in Georgia – had filed applications" for Model Cities funds in early 1967, compared to the 572 US cities that sent representatives to regional Model Cities conferences the year prior.[14] The lack of enthusiasm shocked Washington, but the small number of applicants gave Georgia cities a better chance of acceptance into the program. At the same time, the smaller response fueled conservative criticism.

Attempts to eradicate poverty were not new, but what was new this time was Johnson himself. Louise Lander, in her book *War on Poverty*, claims that what was different about this war was the energy President Johnson devoted to it.[15] The president declared the eradication of poverty to be a national goal in early January of 1965. Later that same month, Johnson proposed his budget to Congress, which allocated nearly one billion dollars of federal funds to antipoverty efforts.[16] Johnson's enthusiasm was unprecedented in the high levels of energy and focus he put towards antipoverty efforts.

Atlanta officials, however, did not seem to have the same enthusiasm Johnson did for ending poverty. The Atlanta program's chief supporters included the local MCP executive director Jonny Johnson and Mayor Ivan Allen, who both worked tirelessly to maintain control over the program and dismiss community participation. Specific grassroots activists expressed their concerns early on. An Atlanta civic group, the Atlanta Metropolitan Grassroots Council (Grassroots Council), asked "Uncle Sam to make sure the city appoints negroes to help run its proposed program."[17] HUD assured the council's president, Clyde Williams, that posts would be filled by local African Americans. Nevertheless, concerns continued to grow and manifest in other ways. The lack of grassroots representation led to an unrepresentative MCP council whose members worked to extend economic aid and end racial segregation, but in doing so, alienated the people it was supposed to serve. As a result, the great expectations President Johnson had for the MCP initiative fell short.

Extending Racial and Economic Segregation

Local officials implemented Atlanta's Model Cities Program in a way that reaffirmed existing patterns of racial and economic segregation. A lack of meaningful and racially diverse community participation in the local Model Cities' Executive Council reinforced the racial divisions experienced by the city's black citizens. This impeded the potential progress of the program and resulted in a racially biased Executive Council. Consequently, the prejudiced council developed racially segregated housing projects. These discriminatory practices were deeply embedded into the foundation of the program. Georgia's congressional representatives then exacerbated the problems of racially segregated housing. Their lack of commitment to pursue the national goals of the Model Cities Program in their own districts increased racial strife and tension between Atlanta residents and policymakers. The failure of Atlanta's MCP stemmed from a lack of grassroots and racial diversity, discriminatory housing practices, and congressmen who reaffirmed biased practices by not pursuing the national agenda at a state level.

African American appointments to the Model Cities Program were minimal and perpetuated themes of racial segregation, much to the local black community's dismay. The Atlanta Metropolitan Grassroots Council expressed concerns regarding this lack of diversity among the board of officials. In an August 1967 article, "Model City Posts Promised Negroes," Art Prine discussed the communications between the Atlanta civic group president and the HUD office representative. Grassroots Council president Clyde Williams "telegraphed the HUD July 27 asking the agency to withhold funds from Atlanta until the city appointed negroes to its model city policy making board," explained Prine.[18] A HUD representative responded to this message by noting that many other cities did not achieve the national racial quota, but assured the group that Atlanta would.[19] This lack of diverse participation resulted in a racially biased Executive Council. With an almost all-white board, black residents had little representation and minimal influence. The council's decisions, made up of the city's political and economic power brokers, went unchallenged. The citizens designed to benefit from this program had no way to communicate their ideas and needs to program officials.

Ramifications of the biased council included extended racial segregation within the housing aspect of the Model Cities Program. The local Atlanta chapter of the NAACP asked HUD secretary Weaver to cut funds for all Atlanta housing and urban renewal projects until these segregation practices ceased.[20] The organization claimed that Atlanta's Model Cities Program policies were designed to entrench and extend segregation, even though federal legislation intended them to uplift poor African Americans. The belief was that integration would create diverse and affluent communities; the result was new housing developments that were little more than refaced slums. When confronted by the NAACP's claims of racial segregation, Mayor Allen agreed. Allen admitted the public housing aspect of the Model Cities began on a segregated basis but argued that strides towards progress had been made. Mayor Allen never clearly identified what in fact these strides were. The NAACP described this example of racial segregation as appalling and even identified the potential for racial strife produced by the inadequate and segregated housing.[21] The segregated housing worsened Atlanta's already existing racial problems, and the progressive ideas promised at the national level went unfulfilled in the community. Local officials saw segregation as an appropriate way for dealing with African American communities. Atlanta officials reinforced racial segregation rather than promote the national agenda of integration.

The lack of community involvement and diversification of the MCP executive board led to a disconnect between local and national officials. Congressman Fletcher Thompson, as one example, was unconcerned about the lack of diversity among the executive planning board. Thompson, like his other white counterparts on the policy board, used his political influence to assure grassroots activists that he was an advocate for their needs. And like other white counterparts, he did not uphold his promises. Thompson originally agreed with the community groups that one African American appointee to the Executive Council was not enough. After two more seats were filled by black city planners, Thompson believed the council's problem was fixed. Thompson stated, "I'm absolutely sure that city officials have made a sincere and conscientious effort to involve Negros."[22] This raises the question, If there was that much participation, why did the HUD only have room for three African American officials? The program's success depended on community involvement and support. When it came to representing his black constituents, Thompson would not get involved. This lack of dedication to constituents and the national agenda had a negative impact on the program's implementation in Atlanta. The lack of black community involvement hindered the program and contributed to disconnect and mistrust between locals and national officials.

The federal program had all the intentions of integration, but this goal was not fully executed at the local level. Executive director Johnson believed Mayor Allen's racially segregated housing plan was flawed but offered no alternative solution. Residents hoped that Johnson, as an African American city planner, would understand their needs. Instead, when asked about open occupancy and integration, Johnson did nothing. Johnson stated at a community-held luncheon that "integration must come" but explained that he would "look to the people" for direction.[23] He failed to address the program's racist flaws. His excuse, when asked by residents, was that integration could not be implemented in the program until it was well established. Integration was not solved prior to the implementation of housing renewal projects in Atlanta, which caused citizens to relinquish support for the racially biased program. Local officials failed to execute the federal aspects of the MCP, like integration, which most appealed to citizens.

Congressional representatives' lack of commitment to national goals only inflamed the problems of housing segregation in Atlanta. Federal legislation dictated that in order to apply for Model Cities funds, cities had to make a conscious effort to include community involvement from the beginning. Atlanta's quota, Prine outlined, "called for at least one negro to be appointed to the Model Cities executive council."[24] Grassroots activists argued that Atlanta's quota of one African American appointee contradicted federal legislation. They claimed that one black board member could not be considered a conscious effort. Their outcry and demand for diversification of the MCP council was not achieved at the local level. The all-white council expected one black man to represent an entire population of African Americans in Atlanta. The racist undertones of this program were visible to locals. The stipulations outlined by the federal government were not enforced or followed by local officials in Atlanta.

Congressman Thompson and other Georgia legislators were content to represent white suburbia, and in doing so, perpetuated the problems of racial and economic segregation even further. As described in a May 19, 1967, publication in the *Atlanta Constitution*, only three representatives supported the low-income rent supplements, an important aspect of the Model Cities Program.[25] If citizens could not have rent aid, they could not afford to live in the new Model Cities areas. Representative Ben Blackburn, who voted against the rent subsidies, justified his vote because the Model Cities Program fell on the "wrong side of the tracks."[26] He claimed it would upset his comfortably white suburban district. The writer of this newspaper article raised interesting points counter to Blackburn's opinions when he wrote, "Is it wise to allow a cauldron of discontent to continue to boil?" Blackburn and other federal representatives were content to let the slum squalor continue and cut rent subsidies. As long as housing developments were barred from their district, representatives did not care about the national agenda of the Model Cities Program. Representatives at the federal level made the problems at the local level worse. Their lack of commitment to the MCP agenda worsened the problems of racial and economic segregation in Atlanta.

Many people noticed the congressmen's lack of commitment to the highly racialized issues surrounding the Model Cities Program and the effect it had at the local level. The slashing of rent subsidies and funding for the Model Cities Programs by Congress was viewed as bigotry by civil rights leaders such as Dr. Martin Luther King Jr. In one statement, Dr. King argued that the congressional vote would "preserve poverty and perpetuate bigotry."[27] He went as far to say that this vote would incite riots and that only Congress was to blame. As Dr. King suggested, this congressional vote would also preserve poverty for both whites and African Americans. In his statement released by the Southern Christian Leadership Conference, he proclaimed that "millions of poor negroes and whites have been slapped in the face for daring to hope."[28] They were told to wait, and now they had nothing to wait for. With no rent aid, if Atlanta residents even wanted to live in the racially segregated housing districts, they no longer could afford to. Georgia representatives and their lack of commitment to black constituents on national issues negatively impacted local goals. When faced with the difficult decision to vote on rent subsidies, Representative Thompson refused to vote on the issue. He was not even present on the House floor.[29] When it came to standing up for Atlanta's most desperate needs, Representative Thompson "copped out."[30] The congressman's lack of commitment to open occupancy, integration, and affordable housing through rent aid gave local officials the opportunity to enact racially and economically biased policies. This "copping out" exacerbated racial and economic segregation at the local level.

The problems with Atlanta's MCP executive council had a significant impact on the success of the program. The lack of meaningful and diverse community participation left the biased council unchecked, which resulted in racially and economically biased program policies. The problems of segregation were then strengthened by white congressmen's unwillingness to work through the problems of the MCP on a local level. Local officials' contempt for their poor black citizens was not accounted for at the national level. The national agenda of the Model Cities Program looked great from afar, but its implementation at the local level in the case of Atlanta failed.

The Battle for Control

A constant battle ensued between local politicians and community grassroots activists over who would control the Model Cities Program. Program officials used the MCP as a way to gain political capital and the poor vote. Once they captured the votes of their poor black citizens, however, they failed to represent their needs. Atlanta policymakers steadfastly maintained control over the program and would not relinquish any power to community groups. Program officials scoffed at and dismissed activists, which alienated entire groups of potential supporters. This conflict between people with power and people without power created insurmountable tension and is one reason the MCP failed in Atlanta.

The officials running the program were more interested in the poor vote than poor Atlantans themselves, and they used the Model Cities Program as a way to maximize their political power. Mack Moore described the Model Cities Program in Atlanta as a program "conceived in infamy – not humanity"[31] and attacked the motives of officials in charge. The whole program, in Moore's mind, was a master political move designed to get votes for politicians. Congressmen and local city officials did not have pure intentions. Moore was not the only concerned citizen. George Boswell mentioned in his article "Extending the War on Poverty" that many citizens wondered if this war was merely political in strategy. There was less concern for the economic well-being of the people and more concern with capturing this segment of the population's vote. "If the war on poverty ha[d] any virtue," Boswell explained, "it is that it [was] designed to help poor people help themselves."[32] After all the money was spent in attempting to elevate the poor, the Model Cities Program only lessened the pain of poverty, but did not eliminate poverty itself. Poor Atlantans could not pick themselves up, as Boswell described, because so many powerful men were working just as hard to keep them down. A mistrust in officials developed due to their impure intentions. Officeholders did not want to help the poor working class; they were just interested in their votes.

Program officials worked to maintain control over the program, which affected citizens' perception of the Model Cities Program. The Atlanta Model Cities Program, designed to help masses of the working poor, left the city's citizens, in Moore's words, "huddled and trembling" and fearful that more of their problems would be "solved."[33] Moore described how increased inflation made more people rich and more people poor. He blamed LBJ in particular by sarcastically thanking him for the poor's "solved" problems. Moore feared voters would cast their lot for the candidate who promised to get them rich, which would broaden the definition of the "working poor."[34] This fear of government aid perpetuated the problems within the Atlanta MCP. Instead of listening to the demands of its targeted communities, the Executive Council, and in particular executive director Johnson, essentially told Atlanta residents: this is what you need, and now your problems are solved. Fear of the federal government was created by local officials. Mistrust was intensified by officials' unwillingness to loosen control, which led to decreased support for the Model Cities Program.

Atlanta officials struggled to maintain control over the program and alienated potential supporters. Atlanta officials despised public participation and refused to let citizens who lived in these areas give community input. The local chapter of the NAACP asked for a meeting with Mayor Allen on March 21, 1967, to which mayor Allen never replied.[35] Once questioned by a journalist from the *Atlanta Constitution*, "Mayor Allen produced a carbon copy of a letter, dated March 23," in which he responded to the NAACP's request for a meeting but "suggested the NAACP leader should first get additional information."[36] The NAACP wanted to be involved and took the first step towards initiating a meeting to which they were denied. Local community groups who represented poor constituents recognized their potential influence over the MCP, but officials would not allow it. Tension among community activists and program officials affected citizen involvement. This battle over who would control the program negatively impacted Atlanta residents. Officials did not allow community involvement from groups like the NAACP, which resulted in limited support for Atlanta's Model Cities initiatives.

Community actors were also dismissed due to false claims by officials who said there was already too much local involvement. Representative Thompson insisted that most major groups were included from the program's beginning.[37] Yet two major groups, the NAACP and the Atlanta Metropolitan Grassroots Council, complained early on that there were not enough black appointees to the executive council. The involvement of these groups would have required officials like Representative Thompson and Mayor Allen to admit they did not know their own people. It would have also required them to relinquish their authority and cave to the demands of the people. Program officials were threatened by these activist groups and ignored their outcry to preserve their political power. By not listening to groups like the NAACP and the Grassroots Council, officials squandered potential cooperation between Model Cities officials and residents of Atlanta. Community groups were seen as a threat, and officials used the claim of too much involvement to exclude these groups and maintain control.

Politicians won, and poor black Atlanta residents lost their best chance for hope. Atlanta officials running the local program had no intention of helping their citizens. They only cared about building and solidifying their political base. Program officials were unwilling to relinquish control and designed a program which benefited themselves rather than poor residents. Local politicians felt threatened by community activists and, as a result, stifled the best chance Atlanta residents had at gaining visibility and representation. Program officials simply wanted to use the Model Cities for their own political gain and, in the process, created a program designed to fail.

Public Dissatisfaction and Alienation

Both black and white citizens responded to the Atlanta Model Cities Program with mistrust. Although the program was designed to engage the public in community projects, Atlanta officials failed to care and to listen to citizens. Program officials alienated residents and, as a result, participation and support for the program was almost nonexistent. A distrust developed between black citizens and officials. The white public also resented anything leading to black gains. The public was dissatisfied, and officials could not recognize that their own policies were what led to this alienation. The lack of support in Atlanta for the Model Cities Program was a huge problem and led to the demise of the antipoverty initiative.

Officials failed to attract residents to meetings and rallies about a program designed to help their community. Citizens were interested in the MCP and became frustrated when their concerns and issues were not addressed. For one particular rally, held by Director Johnny Johnson, 300 people out of an expected 500 came.[38] Johnson remarked how the turnout was disappointing.

At meetings, citizens made known the improvements they wanted but failed to see them put into action. Citizens openly laughed at Johnson when he claimed that 78% of the people living in the Model Cities neighborhoods had benefited from the housing developments.[39] There was no confidence that officials would make these areas anything other than a ghetto. Distrust led to decreased support and involvement from residents. One local news article, "Prosperity Held Key in Elevating the Poor," claimed that citizens, and even other Model Cities officials, blamed Johnson's incompetency.[40] Once community members realized Johnson's plans were full of empty promises, their involvement reflected this. City planners alienated citizens by not addressing their needs, which contributed to a distrust between the two groups.

Officials also blamed the city's black residents for problems faced by the Model Cities Program. MCP Director Johnson criticized those who "made it" out of the slums as the reason for the minimal improvement made in Model Cities housing. After residents moved up the economic ladder, they moved out of the slums. Those who were left behind, asserted Johnson, were left voiceless.[41] If they stayed, claimed Johnson, there would have been more of a demand for improvements. Officials did not know what it was like to live in these soul-destroying places.[42] Johnson could not understand that the problem *was* the Model Cities Program. Johnson blamed the few people who managed to benefit from antipoverty programs as the reason for the collective failure of the Model Cities initiative.

Once citizens knew their voices would not be heard, they no longer participated. One problem the black community wanted to see solved, and which was present in Model Cities housing, was racial segregation. One concerned citizen who frequented the Hungry Club Luncheon[43] asked Johnson at a meeting if open occupancy would be part of the program.[44] Johnson danced around the question. He said the program must be well established before it could start to think of integration. He took the responsibility off of himself and other officials. The Model Cities Program failed to excite public participation because the very officials who ran the program blamed citizens for asking for too much. Officials failed to listen to the problems of the people, and a lack of participation from residents reflected this.

Decreased support from white Atlantans amplified feelings of disdain towards the black public. Many white Americans who initially supported Model Cities, open housing, and other antipoverty programs began to roll back their support. Jim Rankin, of the *Atlanta Constitution*, used public opinion polls to describe this reaction as "White Backlash" and described how it developed in response to Black Power.[45] The white public rejected anything leading to black citizens' advancement. Their decreased support came from a fear that an increase in Black Power would propel African Americans forward and leave white citizens behind. This decreased support mirrored Congress and its cutbacks and elimination of rent subsidies and other programs. Minimal support and lack of white involvement hurt the Model Cities Program. White citizens rolled back their support in an attempt to cut funding for Model Cities and perpetuate poverty in urban areas.

Civil rights leaders were blamed for this lack of white involvement in antipoverty efforts due to their inability to "fight off" Black Power "racism." Rankin stated that the fault lay "with old-guard civil rights leaders" who had "abdicated their leadership to hate-mongering negro racists."[46] Rankin and other white officials justified the decreased support for Model Cities Programs with their claims of racist civil rights leaders. White Americans would not allow this progressive program to help black citizens. Their attack on civil rights leaders prevented black citizens from economic advancement. Racial cooperation could have been achieved in the Model Cities Program, but white citizens would have never allowed it.

White and black citizens viewed the program with mistrust, and as time went on support for the MCP decreased. Program officials alienated black citizens and blamed those who managed to benefit from antipoverty programs for other citizens' perpetual poverty. White citizens also viewed the program with disdain but in a different light. They were unwilling to support black citizens, and their relinquished support undermined the program.

It Was Not Just Atlanta

While Atlanta failed to successfully implement the Model Cities Program at the local level, it was not the only city to fail at this endeavor. Cities such as Los Angeles, California; Richmond, Virginia; and Hopkins Park, Illinois, further exemplify how the Model Cities Program struggled across the nation. A lack of diversification and participation in the program occurred in many cities. Program officials would not relinquish control and constantly fought to maintain political and economic power. Disdain between white officials and black community surveyors also negatively affected participation for the program.

Atlanta's Mayor Allen reflected other US mayors' sentiment about community involvement in antipoverty programs. President Johnson and federal administrators who oversaw local officials pushed for community involvement. However, the program could not be implemented at the local level. While the federal government was still unable to successfully execute the Model Cities Program, they tried to promote diverse participation. Mayor Samuel Yorty of Los Angeles, for example, refused to take the necessary steps to get his city qualified for funds.[47] His refusal contributed to a bloody uprising in August of 1965. After the Watts Riots, however, Mayor Yorty agreed to diversify the MCP Executive Council. In December of 1965, members then included "12 local government officials, 4 officials of private welfare agencies, and 7 representatives from poor neighborhoods."[48] In San Francisco, antipoverty efforts were also stalled by a lack of diversity, and local activists protested the lack of community representatives on the policy board. A compromise was reached and "8 poverty area representatives and 7 city appointees" were placed on the board.[49] Community involvement was stifled. The problems with the lack of diverse participation on executive boards in Atlanta were echoed around the nation.

White officials developed disdain for black community activists. Mrs. G. E. Harris, a social worker tasked with surveying poor Richmond neighborhoods by the local government, was interviewed by the *Richmond Times Dispatch* about the six black female aides who worked for her.[50] These aides were from the communities served by the MCP, and once accepted by fellow residents, they turned into spokeswomen for their neighborhoods. One of the largest concerns the women encountered was the disrespect that residents felt. Harris explained that residents were not respected as individuals. Massing people together created monumental apathy, exclaimed Harris, and she blamed the city planners. These city officials developed disdain towards these aides due to their constant advocacy for these groups and their constant reporting of substandard conditions. City officials' poor planning was brought to light due to these women's work. In an effort to maintain power,

Richmond officials continually discredited these women's findings. Political power was everything, and Richmond officials, like those in Atlanta, demonstrated the desperate attempts made to maintain power.

As in Atlanta, local officials also maintained economic control over antipoverty funds in Richmond. One newspaper article, "Rich Areas Said Getting Biggest Slice of Antipoverty Pie," describes the disproportionate appropriation of antipoverty funds to wealthier areas than to poor ones.[51] Incidents of poverty and the application of resources were not matched in the antipoverty programs. From analysis of per capita income, Barnett concluded that the areas best suited to cope with the problems of poverty on their own were the ones reaping the most benefit from the program. Richmond officials held on to the money and were unwilling to give citizens what they were promised from the federal government.

In Illinois, the black underground newspaper *Independent Voices* described the disconnect and distrust between black officials and citizens. The Office of Economic Opportunity in the Hopkins Park Areas spent $30,000 to "count the number of people living there, survey road conditions, and ask people why they [were] poor."[52] As the editor of the newspaper pointed out in his response to the survey, "Any fool walking or riding around Hopkins Park can see why the people are poor."[53] Employing people to ask citizens why they were poor shows how city and federal officials did not understand the needs of residents. This wasteful use of manpower reflected the disconnect between program officials and citizens. Black citizens who were interviewed developed a disdain towards these surveyors. Surveyors failed to elicit responses because black residents knew nothing would be done.

Conclusion

Atlanta's Model Cities Program failed to be implemented at the local level. Local officials worked tirelessly to maintain power and control and in doing so extended economic and racial segregation. The lack of meaningful and diverse participation led to discriminatory policies passed by the Model Cities Executive Council. The biased program officials used discriminatory practices to disengage community activists and create segregated housing districts. These prejudiced policies were then reinforced by white congressional representatives. These representatives were uncommitted to the national goals of the Model Cities Program, which hurt the local Atlanta program. They were content to represent their white constituents and failed black residents. Local officials also used the Model Cities Program as a way to maintain and reinforce their political power. Officials felt threatened by community activists and used desperate means to control the program. The Model Cities Program was a way for local power brokers to extend their political power and alienate both black and white constituents in the process. The public viewed the program with a deep mistrust and over time relinquished its support for the program. The Model Cities Program was a failure in Atlanta.

The Atlanta Model Cities Program is important because of what it reveals about antipoverty efforts in the 1960s. The Johnson administration passed an incredible amount of legislation, yet still somehow failed to establish a successful antipoverty legacy. Analysis of the Model Cities Program reveals how antipoverty legislature is much more complicated than it seems. In order for a program to be successful, it must be unbiased, supported by both citizens and politicians, and, above all else, pure in its intentions. It was not a failure on the federal government's part to pass legislation in the 1960s but a lack of commitment from local government to the national agenda that caused this program and others like it to flop. Some small victories from the War on Poverty hold true today, but it never achieved its ultimate goal.

Notes

1. Mack A. Moore, "Model Cities 'Conceived in Infamy,'" *Atlanta Constitution*, October 7, 1970, 4A.
2. Moore, "Conceived in Infamy," 4A.
3. Lyndon Baines Johnson, "First State of the Union Address," speech, Washington, DC, January 8, 1964, American Rhetoric, https://www.americanrhetoric.com/speeches/lbj1964stateoftheunion.htm (accessed March 3, 2019).
4. David Farber and Beth Bailey, *The Columbia Guide to America in the 1960s* (New York: Columbia University Press, 2001), 29.
5. Andrew Carswell, "Model Cities Program," in *The Encyclopedia of Housing*, 2nd ed. (Thousand Oaks, CA: Sage Publications, 2011).
6. Carswell, "Model Cities Program."

7. Carswell, "Model Cities Program."
8. Annelise Orleck, *Storming Caesars Palace: How Black Mothers Fought Their Own War on Poverty* (Boston: Beacon Press, 2005), 5. Annelise Orleck, *The War on Poverty: A New Grassroots History, 1964–1980* (Athens: University of Georgia, 2019).
9. Kenneth Heineman, "Model City: The War on Poverty, Race Relations, and Catholic Social Activism in 1960s Pittsburg," *The Historian* 65, no. 4 (2003): 867.
10. Martha Bailey and Sheldon Danziger, *Legacies of the War on Poverty* (New York: Russel Sage Foundation, 2013), 5.
11. Bailey and Danziger, *Legacies of the War on Poverty*, 5.
12. Bailey and Farber, *The Columbia Guide to America in the 1960s*, 28.
13. Bailey and Danziger, *Legacies of the War On Poverty*, 7.
14. Constitution Washington Bureau, "Atlanta's Model City Hopes Rise as Requests Fall Short," *Atlanta Constitution*, May 3, 1967, 11.
15. Louise Lander, *War on Poverty* (New York: Facts on File, 1967), 1.
16. Lander, *War on Poverty*, 9.
17. Art Prine, "Model City Posts Promised Negroes," *Atlanta Constitution*, August 25, 1967, 22.
18. Prine, "Model City Posts Promised," 22.
19. Prine, "Model City Posts Promised," 22.
20. Alex Coffin, "NAACP Here Asks Housing Fund Halt," *Atlanta Constitution*, April 1, 1967, 9.
21. Coffin, "NAACP Asks Fund Halt," 9.
22. Prine, "Model City Posts Promised," 22.
23. "Model City Chief Hopes to Bar Bias," *Atlanta Constitution*, February 15, 1968, 17.
24. Prine, "Model City Posts Promised," 22.
25. "Cop-Out on Capitol Hill," *Atlanta Constitution*, May 19, 1967, 4.
26. "Cop-Out on Capitol Hill," 4.
27. "King Assails Elimination of Rent Aid," *Atlanta Constitution*, May 19, 1967, 14.
28. "King Assails Rent Aid," 14.
29. "Thompson's Stand," *Atlanta Constitution*, May 22, 1967, 4.
30. "Cop-Out on Capitol," 22.
31. Moore, "Conceived in Infamy," 4A.
32. George Boswell, "Extending the War on Poverty," *Atlanta Constitution*, November 25, 1966, 4.
33. Moore, "Conceived in Infamy," 4A.
34. Moore, "Conceived in Infamy," 4A.
35. Coffin, "NAACP Asks Fund Halt," 9.
36. Coffin, "NAACP Asks Fund Halt," 9.
37. Prine, "Model City Posts Promised," 22.
38. "Small Crowd out for Model Cities Meet," *Atlanta Daily*, March 23, 1968, 1.
39. Bill Seddon, "Prosperity Held Key in Elevating the Poor," *Atlanta Constitution*, January 5, 1972, 7A.
40. Seddon, "Prosperity Held Key," 7A.

41. Seddon, "Prosperity Held Key," 7A.
42. Hubert Humphrey, *War on Poverty* (New York: McGraw Hill, 1967), 23.
43. "Model City Chief Hopes to Bar Bias," 17.
44. Ananya Roy, Stuart Schrader, and Emma Shaw Crane, "The Anti-Poverty Hoax: Development, Pacification, and the Making of Community in the Global 1960s," Cities 44 (April 2015): 139.
45. Jim Rankin, "Black Power Turns Around," *Atlanta Constitution*, June 14, 1967, 4.
46. Rankin, "Black Power Turns Around," 4.
47. Louis Cassels, "Despite Quiet Screams, Quiet Success in Many Areas: US Says Poor Must Have Voice in Poverty War; City Hall Howls," *New Journal and Guide*, December 11, 1965, 7.
48. Cassels, "Despite Quiet Screams," 7.
49. Cassels, "Despite Quiet Screams," 7.
50. Louise Ellyyson, "Survey of City Neighborhoods Show Varying Personalities," *Richmond Times Dispatch*, March 28, 1966, 5.
51. David Barnett, "Rich Areas Said Getting Biggest Slice of Antipoverty Program," *Richmond Times Dispatch*, March 26, 1966, 3.
52. "War on Poverty," *Independent Voices*, May 16, 1966, 7.
53. "War on Poverty."

5. Comparing Rivals: Antiwar Protests at the University of Virginia and Virginia Tech

FRANK POWELL

Thomas Jefferson once wrote, "The spirit of resistance to the government is so valuable on certain occasions that I wish it to be always kept alive. It will often be exercised when wrong, but better so than not to be exercised at all."[1] The right to protest the government, as can be discerned from Jefferson, is a deeply entrenched American value that stretches back to the founding of the nation. Yet even though protests have been used throughout American history, no other decade has more claim to the use of protest to resist the will of the government than the 1960s. The fight over the Vietnam War was one of the most divisive struggles in American history, sparking massive protests in every corner of the United States. The bulk of these protests consisted of young college-aged Americans, which made college campuses the epicenter of 1960s activism.

Virtually every state had colleges embroiled in the antiwar movement, and Virginia was no exception. The University of Virginia (UVa) and Virginia Tech (known at the time as VPI, or Virginia Polytechnic Institute) both had to confront the rising unrest of students in regard to the Vietnam War. UVa's main campus, located in Charlottesville, Virginia, had a strong antiwar movement that began as an underground group but slowly took center stage in student consciousness as the war dragged on. Virginia Tech, located in Blacksburg, Virginia, had a similar beginning to its antiwar movement. The movement at Virginia Tech began underground yet, in contrast to UVa, never truly won over the majority of the student population. However, students at both UVa and Virginia Tech were galvanized by the Kent State shootings, which led to outrage and unlawful occupations of campus facilities. Nonetheless, while UVa and Virginia Tech had similar antiwar movements, these movements had differing levels of support.

The majority of historical work done on the antiwar movement argues that while the antiwar movement may have failed in its goal of stopping the war in Vietnam, it had a lasting impact on American society.[2] The movement forever changed political activism and gave a voice to the younger generation of Americans. Many historians also stress the importance of not looking at the movement as one large entity but as a diverse effort that depended on race, college, and geographic location. The vast majority of historical scholarship on the college antiwar movement focuses on the events that transpired on the campuses of elite schools, such as the University of California, Berkeley, and Colombia University, or at public universities in the Midwest and the North. A few historians have looked into southern colleges and their antiwar movements, but for the most part scholarship on this area is lacking.[3] This highlights the fact that the full story of the antiwar protest movement has yet to be told.

This chapter will compare and contrast the antiwar movements on the campuses of the University of Virginia and Virginia Tech. Exploring the similarities and differences between activism at these two universities will not only give additional southern perspectives to what is still an overly northern- and midwestern-focused history, but also provide insight into whether or not the antiwar movement can be seen as a homogeneous entity. Virginia Tech and UVa are separated by a short two-hour drive, but their geographic proximity did not mean that student life at these two schools was the same. The similarities and differences between these two schools will thus tell a lot about not only these particular institutions but about the antiwar movement as a whole.

The University of Virginia and Virginia Tech had two differing antiwar movements because of their divergent histories and political tendencies. Charlottesville has often leaned to the political left and thus is a more progressive city, creating a liberal climate that rubbed off on UVa. The university's antiwar movement was comprised of mainly left-leaning students, and the school's relatively amenable political culture meant that speaking out against the government and the war in Vietnam was a fairly acceptable thing to do. This liberal-leaning mentality differed largely from Blacksburg's outlook. Located in rural southwest Virginia, Virginia Tech has traditionally had much more of a right-leaning political tendency. Right-leaning politics, as well as a strong military tradition at Virginia Tech due to the Corps of Cadets, made it much more difficult for students to garner support for antiwar protests. This chapter will argue that the antiwar movement at UVa had the support of the majority of its students whereas Virginia Tech's antiwar movement was more of a vocal minority. Even among two state universities in the same state, antiwar protests were not uniform.

Throughout the 1960s and 1970s, the youth of America died far from home for a cause that many of them did not believe in. In 1964, North Vietnam attacked two U.S. destroyers in the Gulf of Tonkin, which the United States government used as justification for direct military intervention into Vietnam. At first, the Vietnam War had the support of many Americans due to the public's strong anti-communist sentiment. Yet as the war continued, and with no obvious progress being made, the conflict quickly became unpopular. Politicians in Washington constantly lied to the American public because they promised to bring a swift end to the war, yet let it drag on. As the Vietnam War persisted, more and more young men were forced into the armed forces through the draft. In fact, from 1964 to 1969, the Selective Service System "induct[ed] an average of around 300,000 young men annually" into the United States military.[4] The draft became increasingly unpopular as support for the war effort dwindled, especially among college-aged Americans. The unpopularity of the Vietnam War and the draft led to draft resistance, one of the more controversial aspects of the antiwar movement.[5]

College campuses during the 1960s thus were activist hotbeds for the antiwar movement. Student activists created movements to bring attention to and address various issues they saw as unjust on their campus and around the nation, but the one issue that linked virtually all college protesters together was the war in Vietnam. College-aged Americans were the ones being drafted and sent to Vietnam to fight, so they had the most to lose as the war went on. This tension between students and the government led to a massive antiwar movement that would pit young Americans against the leaders in Washington. Change needed to take place, their voices needed to be heard, and the only way for the youth of America to make sure this happened was through protest.[6]

In order for a protest movement to operate, it must first have a way in which to communicate with other people within the community to pass information and opinions along. At both the University of Virginia and Virginia Tech, the way that the antiwar movements attempted to spread the word of protest and communicate with their student bodies was through the press, specifically through their student-run newspapers. The newspaper used by Virginia Tech activists was known as *Alice*, and the newspaper for the University of Virginia was the *Virginia Patriot* and then later the *Cavalier Daily*.

During the 1960s, the liberal students at Virginia Tech felt alienated by the main campus newspaper, the *Virginia Tech*. The *Virginia Tech* (now known as the *Collegiate Times*) is the long-running student-led newspaper at Virginia Tech. It started as a sports-focused newspaper, but as the paper grew larger it changed and incorporated campus news and opinion pieces.[7] The paper was important to the student population because it was one of the main ways information was spread throughout campus, yet during the spring of 1968 that changed. The *Virginia Tech* had been publishing articles about a developing scandal involving disciplinary action taken by the university administration against four students who were trying to petition to have the school dress code changed, and all of a sudden, coverage of the event stopped.[8] Many students on the liberal side of the political spectrum, the antiwar side, saw this as an attempt by the university, which controlled the *Virginia Tech*'s funding, to prevent the story from getting out. Believing that the *Virginia Tech* had been compromised, these liberal students created their own underground newspaper, known as *Alice*, to broadcast their voices and opinions to the entire student population. In the first issue of *Alice*, the writers stated that the purpose of their paper was to "support views and policies that are felt to be for the promotion of education and the principles upon which this nation was founded."[9] *Alice* writers felt that Virginia Tech was limiting the ability of students to think freely for themselves as human beings.

Throughout its history, *Alice* published many articles that were critical of the Vietnam War, many of which called the war illegal. In one of those articles, John Perrin wrote that "the Vietnam War is illegal. ... All across this land men are being conscripted into a war that was not properly authorized by the Congress of the United States."[10] *Alice* also published an article in May 1970 that supported draft resistance, giving detailed information on how to join a draft resistance movement. The article complained that draft resisters would be "branded felons because they won't support murder" and noted that college students at Virginia Tech "sympathize" with the desire to avoid going to Vietnam.[11] The disdain for the Vietnam War is evident in the rhetoric of

Alice's writers. *Alice* represented antiwar sentiment on campus, and being free to publish its antiwar rhetoric and left-leaning opinions, the newspaper attempted to win over the student body at Virginia Tech.

The majority of students at Virginia Tech, however, did not agree with the rhetoric and sentiments published in *Alice*. *Alice*'s publishing decreased dramatically in late 1969 and by mid-1970 stopped altogether.[12] This is strange considering that, in both 1969 and 1970, activism within the antiwar movement was at an all-time high. *Alice* would not have stopped publishing if it had a large following and readership. This leads one to believe that the ideas written in *Alice* were not popular among the majority of Virginia Tech students, which seems likely considering the fact that no liberal newspaper took up *Alice*'s mantle after it stopped publishing. The reason *Alice* stopped publishing articles and why the *Virginia Tech* refrained from using liberal rhetoric may have been due to the student body not supporting the ideas espoused by the antiwar movement.

The University of Virginia, unlike Virginia Tech, had a more liberal student body that wanted to bring attention to the Vietnam War and the growing antiwar movement. UVa had its own underground newspaper, known as the *Virginia Patriot*, which students founded in 1966 with the goal to "dedicate themselves to various concerns of liberty."[13] The *Virginia Patriot* was similar to Virginia Tech's *Alice* in regard to its left-leaning tendencies. However, the more important comparison is between the *Virginia Tech* (*Collegiate Times*) and UVa's daily newspaper, the *Cavalier Daily*. The *Virginia Tech* did not concern itself with the antiwar rhetoric, yet the *Cavalier Daily* did. On May 1, 1967, for example, the *Cavalier Daily* posted an editorial by U.S. senator Mark Hatfield on its front page, stating that the draft needed to end. Hatfield asserted that "America is overdue in bringing to an end this [the draft] drastic invasion of the lives and liberties of her young men."[14] On September 22, 1969, the *Cavalier Daily* posted another front page article titled "The Vietnam War Must End Now," in which the author, Rob Buford, wrote about a student action movement to protest against the Vietnam War.[15] Articles like Hatfield's and Buford's were constantly front-page news in the *Cavalier Daily*. Front-page news is the most important news, or at least the most important news to the newspaper, and if the *Cavalier Daily* was putting antiwar news on the front page consistently, that says something about its opinion on the issue. The daily newspaper of any school can give insight to what is important to the student body, and from what was on the front page of the *Cavalier Daily* in the 1960s, it seemed that putting an end to the Vietnam War was on the minds of many UVa students. Antiwar protest rhetoric was mainly found in the underground newspaper at Virginia Tech, but by comparison at UVa, it existed in both the underground and main campus newspaper.

Both UVa and Virginia Tech had antiwar protest newspapers in one form or another, yet this was not the only form of antiwar protest that both universities shared. UVa and Virginia Tech both experienced protests against their military programs during the 1960s. Virginia Tech has a long and storied history with the military, due to a Corps of Cadets that has been at the university since its founding in 1872. The University of Virginia, however, has a much younger military program, the Navy ROTC, which was established in 1940. This difference played a role in how students interacted with their respective military training organizations. UVa had less of a military tradition, so students respected the ROTC less than at Virginia Tech, where the Corps had a long-standing tradition. The lack of military custom at UVa, and the strong military practice at Virginia Tech, ultimately shaped the way students responded to protests against their respective organizations.

During the 1960s, there was a lot of animosity towards the Navy ROTC program at the University of Virginia. ROTC programs are designed to prepare and train students for future careers in the military. Therefore, the presence of a military program on campus angered antiwar protesters at UVa since it represented everything they opposed. According to Joseph Fry, "at the height of student protest, 197 ROTC buildings were attacked nationally," and "only a small number of these attacks occurred in the South," and the University of Virginia was on that list.[16] On May 5, 1970, the day after the National Guard shot and killed demonstrating students at Kent State University, over 250 UVa students occupied Maury Hall, the Navy ROTC building, in protest of the Vietnam War and in memory of the Kent State shooting.[17] Students said that their reason for occupying the building was to condemn the "violence in Ohio and the escalation of the Indochina war."[18] The protesters were forced to leave when the police arrived with an injunction, which ordered the protesters to evacuate the building. The occupation of Maury Hall shows that the antiwar movement at UVa viewed the ROTC as a symbol of militarism and believed that having the organization on campus fueled the Vietnam War.

On May 11, 1970, antiwar protesters from the University of Virginia took their protest and message against violence and the escalation of the Vietnam War to Virginia's U.S. senators. The student protesters met the senators in Washington, D.C., and engaged in angry rhetoric with their representatives, making sure that their voices were heard by the people in power. The protesters were also in the midst of voting on a strike resolution that contained nine demands, one of which was the removal of the ROTC program from campus.[19] The demand to remove the ROTC program did not pass, but the mere fact that it was up for consideration shows just how much disdain a large portion of the student body had for anything related to the military and militarism.

Even though the Corps of Cadets had a long-standing tradition at Virginia Tech, there were still antiwar protesters who opposed the idea of having a militarized organization on their Blacksburg campus. Students regularly crowded the Drillfield to protest the war and the Corps of Cadets, which some students saw as a "symbol of the system."[20] The "system" was a phrase that often was understood to be the government or some form of authority figure. Antiwar students fed up with the so-called "system" and the Corps of Cadets' presence on campus decided to take action. On April 15, 1970, a group of these protesters converged on the Drillfield in order to confront the cadets. While the Corps was in the process of a regularly scheduled ROTC drill, the group of antiwar students assembled with the goal of breaking up the drill.[21] In the end, the student protesters were able to accomplish their goal and forced the cadets to flee the Drillfield. This action was not taken lightly by Dr. Hahn, the president of Virginia Tech, who took a hard-line stance against the protesters. Dr. Hahn filed for an injunction to prevent actions similar to that of the protesters on April 15 from happening again on campus. Protests at Virginia Tech and UVa, while having similar circumstances, thus had two different outcomes.

While military programs on college campuses created animosity throughout the student population of America, nothing mobilized student antiwar protesters more than the shooting at Kent State University. In May of 1970, just a few short years after President Nixon had campaigned and won on a promise to "find a quick and honorable way to end the war [in Vietnam]," the United States military invaded Cambodia, further escalating the Vietnam War.[22] This galvanized the student antiwar movement, which led to one of the most infamous events of the antiwar movement, the shooting at Kent State. From May 1–4, 1970, students at Kent State University in Ohio mounted a series of increasingly violent antiwar protests in response to the invasion of Cambodia, which prompted Ohio's governor to call in the National Guard. This was a fateful decision because on May 4, 1970, the National Guard opened fire on a large group of student protesters, wounding nine and killing four.[23] News of this atrocity quickly reached every campus across the United States, sparking outrage and a demand for justice by the student population. Dr. Jerry Lewis, a sociology professor at Kent State University, estimated, in an interview on NPR, that "800 schools closed down" and "over four million students [went] on strike" in reprisal of the shooting, showing just how widespread the protests were.[24] Virginia Tech and the University of Virginia were no exception to this, and students there reacted similarly in the aftermath of the Kent State shooting.

On May 5, 1970, just one day after the shooting at Kent State, 300 Virginia Tech students converged on the house of Dr. Hahn. The students wanted Hahn to cancel classes on May 7 so that students could mourn and memorialize the four Kent State students who were killed. Hahn told the students that he believed that the tragedy at Kent State was a "scar on the conscience of the country" and that he "wanted to do everything in [his] power to avoid that kind of setting, to avoid violence."[25] Yet Dr. Hahn could not give the students the day off without first speaking with the university council. On May 12, 1970, the university council came to a decision and announced in front of Burruss Hall, the main administrative building, that "all regularly scheduled classes and other activities would continue as usual."[26] The decision handed down by the university to not cancel classes outraged the students massed outside of Burruss and prompted them to converge on and occupy another campus building, Williams Hall.

Occupying Williams Hall was a radical move that the students took to have their voices heard, but ultimately it stamped out the antiwar movement on Virginia Tech's campus. The students barricaded the entrances and exits to Williams Hall, not allowing anyone in or out of the building. The occupation of the hall went on through the night of May 12 into the morning hours of May 13. At six o'clock that morning, President Hahn declared the occupation of Williams Hall to be a "considerable hazard to public safety" and called in the Virginia State Police to take control of the situation.[27] The state police gave the students a warning to exit the building or they would come in and remove them; after thirty minutes of noncompliance the police broke through the barricades and dragged the students out of the building. It was reported, by Warren Strother in the *Virginia Tech Telegram*, that more than 100 students were arrested and taken to the Montgomery County Jail in relation to this incident. After the occupation of Williams Hall, Hahn issued a statement that said the students who participated in the protest would have twenty-four hours to collect their belongings from campus, and after that they would be considered trespassers. This was a hard-line stance taken by Dr. Hahn and the Virginia Tech administration against the student protesters in an attempt to stop further incidents like that from occurring in the future.

Dr. Hahn received thousands of letters from students, parents, and people all over the country who heard the news praising his actions against the protesters who had occupied Williams Hall. Lillian Craig, a woman from Norfolk, Virginia, wrote to Dr. Hahn that if more university presidents took the strong stance against student protesters like Hahn had, then "most of the student trouble would end."[28] Frank Caldwell III, a student at Virginia Tech, wrote in another letter to President Hahn that Hahn had the support of "90% of the student body" and the actions of a few students did not represent the majority of the student body.[29] Dr. Hahn, and many Virginia Tech students, took pride in cracking down on dissent to make sure that it did not happen again on campus.

Students at the University of Virginia demanded the same thing Virginia Tech students advocated for in response to the Kent State shooting: a day to memorialize and mourn the dead students while also pointing to the importance of stopping the war in Vietnam. In the wake of the Kent State shooting, there was much unrest on the University of Virginia's campus. On May 6, a general student strike began, backed by the student council, which encouraged students to not go to class in protest. The student council said that "it is time to briefly put academic affairs aside and to discuss matters at hand," the matters at hand being the outrage over Kent State.[30] Student demonstrations broke out all across campus, activists occupied more buildings, and protesters marched down Rugby Road, an area that served as the sorority and fraternity center of campus and is close to the Rotunda, the symbolic center of campus. On May 8, UVa president Edgar Shannon felt forced to call in the police to defuse the situation. Around 200 police officers stormed the lawn at UVa (the center of campus and location of the famous Rotunda) and arrested sixty-eight students to restore order to the campus. The University of Virginia had a much larger student uprising than Virginia Tech did, and thus more officers were needed to quell the uprising.

In the aftermath of the arrest of the 68 students on the lawn, President Shannon gave a speech in front of the Rotunda with over 4,000 students listening. Shannon called for the politicians in Washington to "demonstrate determination to end the unprecedented alienation of the youth."[31] The President stood by his decision to keep the school open, but he told the crowd that he urged professors to make accommodations for students who preferred to be activists and protest the war. In his speech, Shannon criticized the violence police used to break up and arrest protesters. He said the police acted "to a degree I did not expect, and hope to avoid in the future."[32] Shannon pandered to the student population while at the same time attempted to save face by saying class was still on, even though it was seemingly optional after his speech.

President Shannon and President Hahn had two very different approaches to dealing with campus unrest in the wake of the Kent State shooting. Hahn took the hard-handed approach, which was praised by many, and Shannon caved to the will of the student body. A newsletter named the *Sally Hemings Newsletter*, which was given out at the University of Virginia strike committee headquarters after the Kent State shooting, spoke on the contrast between the two schools' Kent State protests, saying:

> Right now, there is a rather ugly comparison being made between U.Va. and V.P.I, and we can guess in the eyes of the Governor's Mansion, the savior of Virginia youth is your hero and ours, T. Marshall Hahn. A quick check of the scoreboard shows Hahn ahead 107 to 68. Not only is Hahn ahead but Mr. Shannon apologized for the high score and told the team how proud he was of their school spirit. ... We don't need a man [Hahn] ... who chalks up brownie points for each student head that is cracked at Tech.[33]

This newsletter shows the divide between what students at UVa thought about Hahn's approach and what they thought about Shannon's. While UVa students were not happy with President Shannon's response to their demands, based upon the amounts of "boos" he received during his speech, they hated what Hahn had done at Virginia Tech even more. Virginia Tech students, on the other hand, seemed happy with the outcome Hahn had produced and more than likely would have hated the chaos that occurred at UVa. While UVa and Virginia Tech had similar circumstances, student responses to the outcomes were vastly different.

The 1960s has become a time in American memory that is clouded and obscured by generalities. Many Americans associate movements, such as the civil rights movement, the antiwar movement, and the counterculture, into one monolithic conglomeration. They believe that everyone in these movements had the same values and the same stories to tell, and that is why they were a part of "the movement." This chapter has compared two public universities that are a short two-hour drive from each other, and while they had similarities, they also had two vastly different antiwar movements on their campuses.

This chapter has compared various aspects of the antiwar movements at UVa and Virginia Tech. At UVa, antiwar rhetoric was virtually everywhere, in the underground newspaper and in the daily student-run newspaper. At Virginia Tech, antiwar rhetoric was kept more under wraps in an underground newspaper. UVa was headed by a much more sympathetic president in President Shannon, which allowed the antiwar movement at the university to run rampant across the campus and take more of a commanding role in public affairs than it could at Virginia Tech. President Hahn was no-nonsense and did not allow for his students to run amok on campus. The two universities also had differing views on how to deal with their military organizations on campus, with UVa taking a vote to completely ban them from campus. UVa's and Virginia Tech's differing antiwar movements illustrate the complexities of 1960s activism.

All of these things contribute to the narrative that the antiwar protest movement on college campuses varied from campus to campus. It is difficult to lump colleges together and assume that they had the same set of values and beliefs, because as this chapter has shown two schools in Virginia were not even the same. Understanding the antiwar movement and the mindsets of the students that led the movements is as important today as it was in the 1960s because American campuses are becoming activist hotbeds once again with the rise of groups like Antifa and the alt-right. Analyzing the similarities and differences between the antiwar movements at Virginia Tech and the University of Virginia adds to the scholarship that the antiwar movement was not unitary, helping to further untangle the confusion that was the 1960s.

Notes

1. "Thomas Jefferson to Abigail Adams," February 22, 1787, in Founders Online, National Archives, https://founders.archives.gov/documents/Jefferson/01-11-02-0182.
2. Michael S. Foley, *Confronting the War Machine: Draft Resistance During the Vietnam War* (Chapel Hill: The University of North Carolina Press, 2003); Mitchell K. Hall, "The Vietnam Era Antiwar Movement," *OAH Magazine of History* 18, no. 5 (October 2004): 13; Kenneth J. Heineman, *Campus Wars: The Peace Movement at American State Universities in the Vietnam Era* (New York: NYU Press, 1993).
3. Joseph A. Fry, *The American South and the Vietnam War: Belligerence, Protest, and Agony in Dixie* (Lexington: University Press of Kentucky, 2015); Andrew Grose, "Voices of Southern Protest During the Vietnam War Era: The University of South Carolina as a Case Study," *Peace and Change: A Journal of Peace Research* 32, no. 2 (2007): 153–67.
4. "Vietnam War Statistics," VIETNAM WAR STATISTICS, April 12, 1997, historyworld.org/vietnam_war_statistics.htm.
5. For more information on the Vietnam War and draft resistance, read: Michael S. Foley, *Confronting the War Machine: Draft Resistance During the Vietnam War* (Chapel Hill: The University of North Carolina Press, 2003); Mitchell Hall, *The Vietnam War* (New York: Routledge, 2018).
6. For more information on college activism, read: Kenneth J. Heineman, *Campus Wars: The Peace Movement at American State Universities in the Vietnam Era* (New York: NYU Press, 1993); Edward P. Morgan, "Political Education: The New Student Left and the Campus Revolt," *The 60s Experience* (Philadelphia: Temple University Press, 1991), 86–126.
7. "About Us," *Collegiate Times* (accessed May 1, 2019), http://www.collegiatetimes.com/site/about.html.
8. Adriennearchivist, "Alice–Virginia Tech's 1960s Underground Newspaper," Special Collections at Virginia Tech, October 10, 2014 (accessed April 2, 2019), https://vtspecialcollections.wordpress.com/2014/10/10/alice-virginia-techs-1960s-underground-newspaper/.
9. Blacksburg Free Press, *Alice*, 1.1, May 18, 1968, 1, VT Special Collections Online (accessed April 2, 2019), https://digitalsc.lib.vt.edu/LD5655.V8 A44/alice_v1n1.
10. Blacksburg Free Press, *Alice*, 6.4, November 1969, 2, VT Special Collections Online (accessed April 2, 2019), https://digitalsc.lib.vt.edu/LD5655.V8 A44/alice_v6n4.
11. Blacksburg Free Press, *Alice*, 8.2, May 1970, 3, VT Special Collections Online (accessed April 2, 2019), https://digitalsc.lib.vt.edu/LD5655.V8 A44/alice_v8n2.
12. Adriennearchivist, "Alice–Virginia Tech's 1960s Underground Newspaper," Special Collections at Virginia Tech, October 10, 2014 (accessed April 2, 2019),

https://vtspecialcollections.wordpress.com/2014/10/10/alice-virginia-techs-1960s-underground-newspaper/.

13. *The Virginia Patriot*, October 3, 1966, Charlottesville: Patrick Henry Society, University of Virginia, 1966, Social Movements Collection, Special Collections Department, the University of Virginia Archives.
14. Mark Hatfield, "Goodby to the Draft," *The Cavalier Daily*, May 1, 1967, https://news.google.com/newspapers?nid=cDbf6tmpe-SoC&dat=19670501&printsec=frontpage&hl=en.
15. Rob Buford, "The Vietnam War Must End Now," *The Cavalier Daily*, September 22, 1969, https://news.google.com/newspapers?nid=cDbf6tmpe-SoC&dat=19690922&printsec=frontpage&hl=en.
16. Joseph A. Fry, "Chapter 7: Southern College Students," *The American South and the Vietnam War: Belligerence, Protest, and Agony in Dixie* (Lexington: University Press of Kentucky, 2015).
17. Peter Shee and Mike Gartian, "Court Ousts Students From ROTC Building," *The Cavalier Daily*, May 6, 1970, 1, https://news.google.com/newspapers?nid=cDbf6tmpeSoC&dat=19700506&printsec=frontpage&hl=en.
18. Peter Shee and Mike Gartian, "Court Ousts Students From ROTC Building," *The Cavalier Daily*, May 6, 1970, 1, https://news.google.com/newspapers?nid=cDbf6tmpeSoC&dat=19700506&printsec=frontpage&hl=en.
19. Helen Dewar, "Va. Students Take Protest to Senators," *The Washington Post*, May 12, 1970, A6.
20. "Text from a Flier That Was Circulated around Campus during April, 1970," *Protest Flyer*, April 1970.
21. Kevin Hunt, "Drill Practice Stopped by Protesting Students," *The Collegiate Times*, April 17, 1970, 1.
22. "Cambodia: Was the U.S. Invasion of Cambodia in May 1970 Justified?," in *History in Dispute*, ed. Benjamin Frankel, vol. 1, *The Cold War: First Series* (Detroit: St. James Press, 2000), 40–47. U.S. History in Context (accessed March 30, 2019), link.galegroup.com/apps/doc/CX2876100015/UHIC?u=imgacademy&xid=57233f40.
23. Chris W. Post, "Beyond Kent State? May 4 and Commemoration Violence in Public Space," *Geoforum* 76 (2016): 142–52.
24. "Kent State Shooting Divided Campus And Country," NPR, May 3, 2010 (accessed April 15, 2019), www.npr.org/templates/story/story.php?storyId=126480349.
25. Robert Back, "300 Students Talk to Hahn," *Collegiate Times* [Blacksburg, V.A.], May 8, 1970, 1.
26. Warren Strother, "VA. State Police Aid in Keeping Order on Campus," *The Virginia Tech Telegram* [Blacksburg, V.A.], June 1970, 1, 7.
27. Strother, "VA. State Police."
28. Lillian P. Craig, "Letter to Dr. Hahn 14 May 1970," May 14, 1970 (Blacksburg, V.A.: Hahn Collection).
29. Frank B. Caldwell III, "Letter to Dr. Hahn 14 May 1970," May 14, 1970 (Blacksburg, V.A.: Hahn Collection).
30. Berry Levine, "Council Backs Strike By Unanimous Vote," *The Cavalier Daily*, May 7, 1970, https://news.google.com/newspapers?nid=cDbf6tmpe-SoC&dat=19700507&printsec=frontpage&hl=en.
31. "Shannon Urges Prompt Action to End War," *The Cavalier Daily*, May 11, 1970,

https://news.google.com/newspapers?nid=cDbf6tmpe-SoC&dat=19700511&printsec=frontpage&hl=en.
32. "Shannon Urges Prompt Action to End War."
33. "Sally Hemings Newsletter," Social Movements Collection, Special Collections Department, The University of Virginia, https://explore.lib.virginia.edu/exhibits/show/sixties/walkthrough/protest.

6. SNCC Identity: From Interracial Nonviolence to Black Power

KAYLA MIZELLE

> The white people coming into the movement cannot relate to the black experience, cannot relate to the word black, cannot relate to the nitty gritty, cannot relate to the experience that brought such a word into existence, cannot relate to chitterlings, hog's head cheese, pig feet, ham hocks, and cannot relate to slavery, because these things are not a part of their experience.
>
> – Student Nonviolent Coordinating Committee position paper, 1966[1]

In the first week of May 1966, staff members from the Student Nonviolent Coordinating Committee (SNCC) attended a meeting that would change the organization for the remainder of its history. Long discussions ensued in the week-long staff meeting over the direction of SNCC and who would lead this militant student wing of the civil rights struggle. During this week, staff members elected Stokely Carmichael to replace John Lewis as chairman. Lewis had been chairman for the past three years, worked closely with Dr. Martin Luther King Jr., and was a champion of nonviolent protest and an interracial vision of equality. Carmichael, in contrast, was uninterested in integrating black Americans into white society. Instead, he advocated for what can be called "radical racial identity": a militant racial separatism that rejected the integrationist, reconciliationist racial framework of the pre-1964 years. It was separatism based on black pride and a refusal to lose one's distinct racial identity by integrating into the dominant white society. Carmichael's election was thus a pivotal moment in SNCC's history that marked the tension the group experienced regarding the shift toward radical racial identity.

The tone of the quote above is closely connected to the dissatisfaction that many SNCC members felt about white participation in the civil rights movement. However, black activists had not always felt this way about their white allies. For part of its life span, SNCC members saw white activists as a potent political tool and encouraged them to join the movement. As the organization aged, however, a new form of radical racial identity emerged. The quote above, from the heart of the discussions on SNCC's new direction on radical identity, was never fully endorsed by the organization, but it circulated widely around SNCC's Atlanta project office. While SNCC was not originally founded as a black-only organization, it became evident to many that white activists could not relate to the black experience as it evolved. It thus became necessary for the group to become racially exclusive in order to focus on its own identity.

SNCC was founded in April 1960 as a student organization under the guidance of leaders from the Southern Christian Leadership Conference. The organization existed from 1960 to 1968 with a mission to create racial equality and reconciliation through nonviolent means.[2] With nonviolence at the heart of the organization, SNCC participated in countless protests, including multiple forms of sit-ins, kneel-ins, boycotts, and marches. SNCC originally focused on gaining civil rights for black Americans; however, it also worked internationally and helped people around the world gain their own civil rights. As an organization, it was at the forefront of the movement and played a crucial role in the passage of the Civil Rights Act of 1964 and the Voting Rights Act of 1965. In the aftermath of these victories, the group continued to work to further racial justice and found a new focus in radical racial identity.

There are two ways in which most authors write about SNCC's identity shift: the first focuses on the consequences that this shift had, and the second pinpoints the moments when it believed this shift occurred. Two authors make arguments for what consequences the shift in identity had on the movement. For instance, Faith Holsaert in her book, *Hands on the Freedom Plow: Personal Accounts by Women in SNCC*, writes about how SNCC women fit into the identity-shift narrative. She outlines the general timeline of the group's rhetorical shift and notes that the female SNCC members who contributed to the book disagree on whether or not white activists should have been expelled from the movement. As she notes, some contributors felt that the consequence of the continued white presence in SNCC would have limited its internal power.[3] Jennifer Wallach in her article "Replicating History in a Bad Way? White Activists and Black Power in SNCC's Arkansas Project," speaks directly about SNCC's shift to black power. Her primary point is that the consequence of the shift killed the idealized view of assimilation into white culture for the entirety of the civil rights movement.[4] The authors who have written about this topic also have a difference in opinion regarding what pinpoint moments caused the shift toward radical identity. For instance, Kwame Jeffries in his article "SNCC, Black Power, and Independent Political Party Organizing in Alabama, 1964-1966" asserts that the shift came from the Lowndes County Freedom Organization. However, Francis Shor in her article "Utopian Aspirations in the Black Freedom Movement: SNCC and the Struggle for Civil Rights, 1960-1965" argues that the shift did not happen at one moment, but that gradually, as the movement progressed, the shift became inevitable.[5] The authors who have written about SNCC discuss two aspects of SNCC's identity, the consequences of the shift and the pinpoint moments the shift occurred.

This chapter specifically focuses on SNCC's shift in radical racial identity from 1960 to 1968. In the early years, the organization's primary goal was to nonviolently advocate for equality and civil rights of all people, black and white. As such, racial identity was not at the forefront of discussion or concern. Activists assumed that once civil rights were achieved, then the process of racial reconciliation and assimilation could begin. However, when the Civil Rights Act was passed in 1964, SNCC began to emphasize defining a separate black identity. Finally, Stokely Carmichael's election as chairman in 1966 signified the end of the utopian experiment in nonviolent interracial relations and a shift toward black power. How did SNCC deal with questions of identity during these three distinct eras? How did SNCC's rhetoric on radical identity evolve? By tracing the organization's writings and thoughts and identifying the moments when this shift occurred, this chapter identifies what events aided the rhetorical shift on radical identity.

Where Did SNCC Come From?

In 1960, the civil rights movement was already in full swing. The Southern Christian Leadership Conference (SCLC) was one of the driving forces of the movement and was deeply committed to nonviolence. The SCLC led multiple movements to fight against the Jim Crow laws of the South that prevented black Americans from enjoying the same public spaces as whites. Although the SCLC was the preeminent civil rights movement at the time, the sudden rise of the student sit-in movement in the winter of 1960 took the organization by surprise. One notable sit-in occurred in Greensboro, North Carolina, when four black students occupied a racially segregated Woolworth's lunch counter. The movement disrupted Woolworth's business and, even more importantly, the civil rights movement as a whole, as it quickly gained traction and spread beyond Greensboro to include student protestors across the South.[6] Through the sit-in movement, black students proved they were unwilling to fall victim to Jim Crow Southern segregation and disrupted the primarily older, adult-run civil rights movement.

The lunch counter sit-in movement caught the attention of Ella Baker, the executive director of SCLC. She saw the impact the young students had and wanted to organize more students to help drive the civil rights struggle. In April 1960, just a few months after the Greensboro sit-in, she, along with Dr. Martin Luther King Jr., organized a conference for student civil rights activists in Raleigh, North Carolina. The conference focused on nonviolent protest movements and empowered students to take action on their own.[7] The result was the creation of the Student Nonviolent Coordinating Committee (SNCC). From the very start, SNCC dedicated itself to nonviolence and protesting for equal rights for all Americans.

Identity in the Years of 1960–64

In the beginning, SNCC had firm roots in a commitment to gaining the equality of all people through nonviolent protest. The group's original objective was not to define and live out radical racial identity but instead to organize students together in an effort to achieve equal rights for all. In the early years of SNCC, the organization preoccupied itself with protesting for equal rights and did not address the matter of black identity. The activists originally protested racial segregation through the lunch counter sit-in movements and the Freedom Rides. However, as integration occurred, SNCC's focus moved to voting rights.[8] SNCC helped make large advances in the fight for civil rights in the years between 1960 and 1964, all of which contributed to the eventual passage of the Civil Rights Act in 1964 and the Voting Rights Act in 1965. The group saw these legislative victories as major accomplishments and expected their implementation to make a change. At the time, SNCC members believed that gaining civil rights for black Americans would make racial differences irrelevant and make assimilation into white culture naturally happen.

SNCC was not founded originally as an organization for black identity. Its founding statement made no mention of it and instead focused its attention on nonviolence and reconciliation. Dr. Martin Luther King Jr. and the SCLC, which were both most well known for their continued unrelenting support of nonviolent protest, played a key role in SNCC's creation. SNCC's founding statement from the Youth Leadership Conference of 1960 (SNCC's founding conference) reflects this influence by stating, "We affirm the philosophical or religious ideal of nonviolence as the foundation of our purpose, the presupposition of our faith, and the manner of our action."[9] As the quote illustrates, the group's fundamental purpose and contribution to the movement began with students dedicated to nonviolent protests for equality. The document continues by adding that nonviolence would lead to reconciliation.[10] From SNCC's very first statement of its purpose it is obvious that fostering a separate black identity was not the group's most important issue; instead its goal was reconciliation through nonviolence.

During its early years, SNCC did not define black identity as a priority because the group felt that achieving equality would naturally lead to reconciliation. SNCC took ideals from the founding statement and wrote a statement of purpose to the platform committee of the Democratic National Convention. The statement explained that the activists' mission was to ensure equal treatment of all people and take direct action against discrimination. SNCC explained exactly what the mission of the organization was by stating, "The question has been asked, 'What do Negro students want?' Our answer is firm and clear: we want all the rights, opportunities, and responsibilities enjoyed by any other American, no more, no less."[11] The position paper went on to identify four areas in which there was inequality: education, employment, voting, and legal protection.[12] SNCC members were not calling on the Democratic National Convention to take drastic measures; they were only asking for support of the rights they should have already been receiving as Americans.

The members of SNCC initially and wholeheartedly viewed nonviolence as the path to equality and believed that if nonviolence was lost, their mission would be lost as well. In October of 1960, a letter written to the editor of SNCC's newsletter, *The Student Voice*, discussed what nonviolence meant to SNCC. The letter began with a discussion of how white Southerners feared the change coming because it meant that their world was falling apart. The U.S. South had been built on racism, and SNCC's goal for civil rights threatened the social, economic, and political structure. According to the author of the letter, nonviolence would be the healer because it would give everyone personhood.[13] The letter failed to address the issue of black identity but did advocate for nonviolence to create a commonality of personhood among all people. SNCC believed that through nonviolence, the equal treatment of all people was possible, and if all people were treated as equals, then the idea of difference would be eradicated. The letter also stated, "If we lose sight of this basic concept of nonviolence, no matter how nonviolent our external tactics remain, we will lose the ultimate potential of the student movement."[14] The author believed that without a strict dedication to interracial nonviolence, the organization would not further the effort for civil rights.

Similarly, an article later in the same issue of *The Student Voice* predicted two possible threats to the movement, the loss of love and violence. Brewster Kneen in his *Student Voice* article "Nonviolence and Vision" wrote, "It is not wrong to seek a resolution to the very severe injustice of segregation but when men take up the way of reconciliation, there are no longer limits to their self-identification; there are no longer simply exploited Negroes; but members of the family of man."[15] Kneen argued that black Americans should want justice for their mistreatment but should seek it in a nonviolent manner that promotes reconciliation. This article is unique in that it referenced identity; however, it is very different from the separate black identity that drove SNCC later in the movement. In this article, Kneen argued that identity would come from nonviolent reconciliation with white people and that through reconciliation black people would gain equal rights.

The 1961 Freedom Rides provide another example of how SNCC prioritized equality and reconciliation as its goals. Following the mass arrests and mob violence of the Freedom Rides, SNCC wrote a telegram to President John F. Kennedy urging him to act on the situation. This telegram asserted that black Americans were first-class citizens and should be treated as such, especially on the interstate bus system. It called for the president to make a statement either for or against the Freedom Rides protest.[16] The Freedom Rides and the telegram to Kennedy were both examples of how SNCC was not focused on racial identity; the primary goal in the early years of the group instead was to gain equal treatment for black Americans. It was assumed through equality that black Americans would be able to reconcile and assimilate with white Americans. Defining black identity was not a priority and was possibly antithetical to the overall goal of equality. Moreover, it was assumed that through the work of protesting, reconciliation and assimilation would occur once civil rights were gained.

SNCC organizers, like Fannie Lou Hamer, prioritized gaining the right to vote and did not focus on black racial identity because they were genuinely suffering without that right; everything else was secondary. Hamer wrote a letter in 1963 to SNCC's northern supporters asking for financial and material aid for those struggling in the South. In this letter she described her own experiences as a supporter of the movement for first-class citizenship. She explained that, as a result of trying to register to vote, she lost her job and had to leave her home. She wrote to her supporters and explained her dissatisfaction with the many injustices she experienced, including having her children go hungry, being beaten and jailed, and being treated as a second-class citizen.[17] She wrote all of this to gain material support from northerners, but it also demonstrates that black identity was not SNCC's primary focus during its early years. Fannie Lou Hamer's experience exhibited what really mattered to SNCC at the time: gaining basic human rights and equal treatment.

Identity in the Years of 1964–66

The Civil Rights Act of 1964 brought an end to one era of SNCC's work as the group changed its focus. Before the passage of this legislation, the group had devoted the bulk of its efforts to the integration of public places. However, the Civil Rights Act made segregating public places illegal. SNCC won and could refocus the organization. And as the activists turned their attention to voting rights, discussions of organizational restructuring also brought up a new conversation about racial identity. In the early years of SNCC, the organization had a pin that depicted a black and white hand shaking each other. However, in 1965 SNCC phased it out.[18] While some might say that the pin was insignificant, dropping visible interracialism as a symbol of the organization says something about the change the group was undergoing. In 1965, the activists no longer thought of the white and black handshake as a symbol that represented the organization, proving that the group was moving towards something new.

The 1964 Freedom Summer campaign played a pivotal role in introducing discussions of racial identity to the group because the influx of white volunteers made black activists realize racial differences needed to be addressed rather than hidden under a blanket of equality. John Lewis, in a 1973 interview, described the beginning of his split with SNCC and attributed it to Freedom Summer. Lewis said the split started with the Freedom Summer's plan to integrate the organization. SNCC integrated in Mississippi by bringing in a large number of new black and white volunteers to aid in the voting registration effort. Lewis felt this integration created numerous problems for SNCC. He said that when the white students arrived from up north, attention went to them instead of to the black students who had been working in the area for several years. To make this clearer to the interviewer, Lewis gave an example of how a young black typist, who could type relatively fast, was replaced by a white girl who could type even faster. He explained this caused a disturbance among the organization, which led to division.[19] This account from John Lewis proved SNCC had internal conflict surrounding the place of white volunteers within the organization. It is evident from the Freedom Summer campaign, which utilized both black and white students, that racial differences in SNCC needed to be discussed. Previously, these differences could be overlooked through the lens of equality, but now that legal equality had arrived, they had to be discussed.

Following the passage of the Civil Rights Act, SNCC spent time thinking more introspectively, which led its members to create a separate black organization and black identity. This is demonstrated in Charlie Cobb's position paper from the Waveland, Mississippi, conference in 1964. Cobb wrote about the types of SNCC people in one section of "On Snick Revolution and Freedom." He described people such as Carmichael, Ivanhoe Donaldson, and James Forman as the "strong people" or the ones everyone wanted to be like. He described the next group as the "freedom highs," the white intellectuals who could never be like the "strong people" because they were not black. He continued to describe this group "and, their role as supplements to the work of the 'strong people.' it sort of ties into the white-black question (which has simply taken another shape) and the need to have a black run and controlled organization."[20] This matters to the rhetoric because it shows the beginning of a desire for a separate black organization and a separate black identity. Cobb felt white members of the organization could not contribute as much as prominent black members and could only supplement their efforts. He also felt there was a division among SNCC and thought the organization should be run and controlled by black activists. The fact that his position came from the Waveland Conference also matters because at this conference the debates on racial roles formed.[21] While this is just one small position paper, it is extremely important because it shows the early ideas of a separate black organization and a separate black identity at a conference over what to do next following the passage of the Civil Rights Act and the Freedom Summer project of 1964.

Towards the end of John Lewis's time as chairman, his own views on radical racial identity also evolved. In February 1965, Lewis spoke to SNCC staff members after he returned to the U.S. from a two-month trip to Africa. He spoke about the similarities he saw between segregation and exploitation in the U.S. South and colonialism in Africa. He continued his speech by speaking on SNCC's current achievement and the progress that had been made. However, then his speech shifted and focused on black identity. John Lewis said,

> Too many of us are too busy telling white people that we are now ready to be integrated into their society. When we make appeals for active, moral, and financial support they have been geared toward the white community and for the most part not at all toward the black community. This is true of all the major civil rights organizations including SNCC. We must dig deep into the black centers of power throughout this nation not just for financial reasons but as a base of political support. I am convinced that this country is a racist country. The majority of the population is white and most whites still hold to the a master-slave mentality.[22]

Stokely Carmichael felt that integration and assimilation into white culture was not an option for black Americans. While John Lewis and Carmichael are normally pitted against each other, this quote shows that at this time, their ideas may have been similar. While Lewis was not calling for the expulsion of white volunteers, he, like Carmichael, no longer believed in the idealized view of interracial equality. Now that the Civil Rights Act had been passed, the ideas of integration from the early years of SNCC were recognized as utopian and unrealistic by members and leaders. This is important because even John Lewis, who closely aligned with Dr. Martin Luther King Jr.'s vision for SNCC, began to call for a new black identity in the movement.

The period between utopian assimilationism and black power was a time of transition for SNCC. The time between 1964 and 1966 forced activists to discuss racial identity. While the group had not begun using the term "black power," it is evident that the organization was moving in the direction of separate black identity and an exclusively black organization. SNCC had been founded on the utopian idea that through equality black Americans would be able to reconcile and assimilate into white America. However, after equality was achieved through the 1964 Civil Rights Act, SNCC activists realized that defining black identity would be the next step for the organization.

Identity in the Years of 1966–68

In 1966, Stokely Carmichael replaced John Lewis as SNCC's chairman and ushered in a new wave of radical racial identity. Lewis's 1973 interview discussed Carmichael's election and the reasons why Lewis ultimately left SNCC. In May of 1966, Carmichael informed Lewis that he would be running for chair of the organization.[23] A report on SNCC and the roots of black power described the "week long meeting near Nashville, Tennessee. They tried to define their position on some basic questions and elected new officers." The report concluded by noting that Lewis had been replaced by Carmichael.[24] Lewis said in the interview that the meeting "went through this long drawn-out debate for many many hours–from about 7:30 P.M. to about 4:00 A.M.–just on and on during that night about the whole question of my relationship with Dr. King, relationship with the White House, Lyndon Johnson, and the whole question of blackness. And the election was reheld and Stokely got the majority of the votes." Lewis lost this election because of his relationship to MLK's vision of nonviolence and his views on black identity. With the election of Carmichael, SNCC was ready to move towards a new radical racial identity.

Lewis recalled the immediate impact Carmichael had on the movement when he used the phrase "black power." As Lewis explained, a few weeks after Carmichael was elected, the James Meredith March Against Fear took place.[25] The march, started by the pioneering integrationist James Meredith, was designed as a stand against the fear black Americans felt registering to vote. Meredith planned to go from Memphis, Tennessee, to Jackson, Mississippi, but a violent attack left Meredith shot in the leg and threatened to bring the march to an early end. In response, many civil rights organizations, including SNCC, continued Meredith's march. As a sign that things were changing, the leading figures on this march, which included King and Carmichael, disagreed about whether protests should be peaceful or not. And it was during this march that Carmichael first articulated a "black power" agenda.[26] Lewis described this development in his interview, arguing that the phrase "black power" was just a chant, but it sparked fear in many whites and cost the civil rights movement a lot of support.[27] The interview demonstrates how, as Carmichael took over SNCC, the organization underwent radical changes in 1966, including in its ideas about race.

With Carmichael's election and his coining of the phrase "black power," it became necessary for SNCC to publicly define its ideas about radical racial identity. Following the group's election-week meetings, Ivanhoe Donaldson, a prominent SNCC leader, gave a speech to the staff members at its May conference. His speech addressed the direction of the group as it moved to what he described as a "critical period." Donaldson explained that "with the passage of the Civil Rights Bill, the Voting Bill, the Economic Opportunity Act, the Supreme Court Ruling on Reapportionment, our system has begun to muddle and make hazy issues we fought so hard to clarify."[28] Donaldson felt that even though America had made progress through legal action, black Americans had not seen these advances implemented. He continued by calling for SNCC to understand black nationalism and its positive impact on the world. Then he called upon white organizers to work in white communities, teach black history, and organize around black needs.[29] His speech made it clear that SNCC was headed in a new direction, one that took it beyond its original integrationist ethos.

SNCC Identity | 97

Donaldson's speech demonstrated that SNCC leaders believed the group had to redefine itself as an organization, even if it was not as explicit as the internal position paper "The Basis of Black Power." This document, quoted at the beginning of this chapter, asserted that white volunteers could not relate to the black experience and that their purpose in the movement had been fulfilled. Therefore, it called for making SNCC a home exclusively for black activists, a place where they could continue to push the movement's efforts, but working from a black separatist framework.[30] Donaldson's speech and "The Basis of Black Power" position paper together demonstrate the shift to radical racial identity that occurred within SNCC after Carmichael's election.

Radical racial identity in SNCC meant that whites would be excluded from the movement. In early December 1966, SNCC staff held a week-long meeting intended to address a wide range of topics, but the question about whether or not white activists should be expelled from SNCC controlled the floor.[31] Comments from Bill Ware at the meeting demonstrated why SNCC believed it had to become a solely black organization. The comments explained that if SNCC was not a solely black organization, then it did not understand the meaning of black power. Ware felt the presence of whites in SNCC would devalue the power of black activists to organize around their racial experiences and identity. He believed that only black people had the ability to tear down racism in America.[32]

The shift to black power also meant that SNCC would no longer commit itself to nonviolence, as it had in the years prior to Carmichael's election. A *Los Angeles Times* newspaper article from 1967 covered the group's shift away from nonviolence. The article went into detail about changes in the organization and addressed SNCC's history of nonviolence starting with MLK. It noted that the group had taken on a new model of black power and had made Malcom X, rather than King, its new role model. And it attributed the radical change in the organization to the shift in leadership from Lewis to Carmichael.[33] In a *Washington Post* article around the same time, Carmichael wrote, "I tried it (nonviolence) for five years and now he (a policeman) is no longer going to beat his humanity into my head. If he touches me, I'm going to kill him."[34] SNCC was a different organization after its rhetoric shifted to black power: it no longer saw a need for white members, nor did it see value in maintaining nonviolence.

As chairman of SNCC, Carmichael explicitly made black power a priority for the group. Carmichael wrote an article for the *New York Book Review* following 1966 as a way of affirming his position on black power in the organization. In this article he wrote, "This is the significance of the black power as a slogan. For once, black people are going to use the words they want to use—not just the words white people want to hear."[35] Carmichael made one of SNCC's main goals as an organization to define and uphold black power. Later in the article, he addressed his opinions on integrating black people into white society. In the early years of SNCC, this was the assumed goal of the organization. However, Carmichael then felt that integration was not only impossible but it was also not what black Americans should want. He described how the idea of "making it" in the black community had become leaving the black community behind and integrating into white America. He complained that in order for blacks to have a "decent house or education," they had to move into white communities. As he argued, this mindset reinforced the racist view that white was inherently better than black.[36] Carmichael's thoughts on integration were an example of why SNCC moved towards black power. To Carmichael, black power meant black people should invest in their communities and work to improve their experience, separate from whites.[37]

Carmichael also gave speeches that effectively explained why black power was necessary and needed support from the black community. In his Watts Speech of November 26, 1966, Carmichael said, "Now the most important thing that black people have to do is to come together, and to be able to do that we must stop being ashamed of being black. This country has made us hate ourselves; this country has made us anti-black."[38] Carmichael wanted his black audience to realize that a separate racial identity was not only necessary but healthy. He wanted his audience to feel proud to be black so that they could move the black freedom struggle forward.

Carmichael wanted black Americans to be proud to be black and take ownership of their communities. He also spoke of black consciousness. In a speech he gave at the University of Puerto Rico, he defined black consciousness as "knowledge of and pride in our identity as Afro-Americans—is therefore part of what we mean by black power."[39] Carmichael felt that in order for black power to successfully eliminate the racist white power structure in America, blacks had to have a sense of pride in their racial identity.[40] Carmichael was the driving force behind SNCC's transition to black power, and he did this by calling on black people to be proud of being black and to work to improve black communities instead of leaving them behind.

SNCC did not last long under the leadership of Stokely Carmichael. The organization had been founded on nonviolence and interracialism yet was no longer committed to either, and it fractured. Carmichael closely aligned himself with the Black Panther Party and wanted to merge SNCC with the Panthers. However, not all SNCC members were keen to the merge, so in 1968, Carmichael left SNCC. As a newspaper article from the *Washington Post* notes, without Carmichael's leadership, the group was falling apart.[41] The organization was split over the support of the Black Panther Party. Carmichael felt the Panthers were the next step in black power. However, some members felt SNCC could not fully support the Panthers because SNCC was nonviolent, while the Panthers' extremists advocated for violence. While the two organizations did not merge until 1968, under the leadership of James Forman, SNCC supported and formed an alliance with the Panthers.[42] In 1969, the SNCC that existed throughout the 1960s finally ended. What was left of the organization could no longer commit to nonviolence, and in 1969 SNCC changed the group's name to the Student National Coordinating Committee.[43]

Conclusion

This chapter explores SNCC's rhetoric on radical racial identity through three key time periods. The organization was founded on the principles of nonviolence, so in the early years between 1960 and 1964, SNCC focused on achieving equality for black Americans through organizing nonviolent protest. The group was preoccupied with organizing for basic civil rights, and radical racial identity was not a primary goal. Instead, most members believed that once civil rights were gained, utopian assimilationism would take shape. However, with the passage of the Civil Rights Act in 1964 and the Voting Rights Act in 1965, activists had to evaluate where the movement was headed next. In the time between 1964 and 1966, the organization had no choice but to begin discussing radical racial identity. SNCC phased out the symbols that once represented the organization, such as the black and white handshake pin used from 1962 to 1965, because they no longer appropriately represented the organization. Finally, this chapter identified the last period of the organization from 1966 to 1968, which focused on the direction Stokely Carmichael took SNCC as chairman. When Carmichael took office, the movement shifted in three short weeks to black power as an expression of radical racial identity. As the black power movement stirred in the organization, maintaining nonviolence began to seem impractical, which led the group to change its name and thus signified the end of the familiar SNCC.

The shift in SNCC's rhetoric from interracial nonviolence to black power matters because it was a part of the larger history of identity movements during the 1960s. SNCC members fought to make huge strides towards the achievement of equality in the early years of the organization, only to find that these advancements would never be properly implemented and would result in black Americans giving up their culture. The group's rhetorical shift proved that equality was not enough. Black Americans wanted equal rights and freedom, but they also wanted to be able to enjoy those rights without losing their voice or culture. SNCC, as a part of the larger black freedom struggle, inspired many other minority groups to speak out against assimilating into white America and to instead take ownership of their own cultural heritage.

Notes

1. SNCC Atlanta Project, "Basis of Black Power," 1966, Veterans of the Civil Rights Movement, https://www.crmvet.org/docs/blackpwr.htm (accessed February 27, 2019).
2. SNCC, "Student Nonviolent Coordination Committee Founding Statement," 1960, Veterans of the Civil Rights Movement, https://www.crmvet.org/docs/sncc1.htm (accessed February 27, 2019).
3. Faith S. Holsaert, *Hands on the Freedom Plow: Personal Accounts by Women in SNCC* (Urbana: University of Illinois Press, 2010).
4. Jennifer Wallach, "Replicating History in a Bad Way? White Activists and Black Power in SNCC's Arkansas Project," *The Arkansas Historical Quarterly* 67, no. 3 (2008): 268-87 (accessed February 21, 2019).
5. Francis Shor, "Utopian Aspirations in the Black Freedom Movement: SNCC and the Struggle for Civil Rights, 1960-1965," *Utopian Studies* 15, no. 2 (2004): 173-89 (accessed February 21, 2019).
6. "Greensboro Sit-In," History Channel, https://www.history.com/topics/black-

history/the-greensboro-sit-in (accessed April 15, 2019).
7. "Founding of SNCC," 1960, SNCC Digital, https://snccdigital.org/events/founding-of-sncc/ (accessed April 17, 2019).
8. SNCC, "You Can Help (friends of SNCC guide)," 1964, Veterans of the Civil Rights Movement, https://www.crmvet.org/docs/640000_sncc_fos.pdf (accessed March 25, 2019).
9. SNCC, "Founding Statement."
10. SNCC, "Founding Statement."
11. SNCC, "Statement Submitted by the Student Nonviolent Coordinating Committee to the Platform Committee of the National Democratic Convention," 1960, Veterans of the Civil Rights Movement, https://www.crmvet.org/docs/6007_sncc_demconv-platform.pdf (accessed March 25, 2019).
12. SNCC, "Statement Submitted by the Student Nonviolent Coordinating Committee."
13. "Across the Editor's Desk," *The Student Voice*, October 2, 1960.
14. "Across the Editor's Desk."
15. Brewster Kneen, "Nonviolence and Vision," *The Student Voice*, October 1960, 3, 4.
16. Edward B. King Jr., "SNCC Wires President Kennedy," *The Student Voice*, April and May 1961, 1.
17. Fannie Lou Hamer, "Letter from Fannie Lou Hamer," 1963, Veterans of the Civil Rights Movement, https://www.crmvet.org/docs/hamer_letter.pdf (accessed March 29, 2019).
18. "Pins of the Freedom Movement," 1962–1965, Veterans of the Civil Rights Movement, https://www.crmvet.org/info/pins.htm (accessed March 29, 2019).
19. Jack Bass and Walter Devries, "John Lewis Interview Transcript," 1973, Documenting the American South, https://docsouth.unc.edu/sohp/A-0073/A-0073.html (accessed February 27, 2019).
20. Charlie Cobb, "On Snick Revolution and Freedom," 1964, Veterans of the Civil Rights Movement, https://www.crmvet.org/docs/6411w_cobb_srf.pdf (accessed March 29, 2019).
21. Veterans of the Civil Rights Movement, "SNCC Conference, Waveland MS," 1964, Civil Rights Movement Documents, https://www.crmvet.org/docs/waveland.htm (accessed March 29, 2019).
22. John Lewis, "Statement to SNCC Staff people," 1965, Veterans of the Civil Rights Movement, https://www.crmvet.org/docs/650200_sncc_lewis_staffmeeting.pdf (accessed March 29, 2019).
23. Bass and Devries, "John Lewis Interview," 59.
24. SNCC, "The Roots of 'Black Power,'" 1966, Veterans of the Civil Rights Movement, https://www.crmvet.org/docs/660000_sncc_bpwr_roots.pdf (accessed March 29, 2019).
25. Bass and Devries, "John Lewis Interview," 59.
26. Tina Ligon, "'Turn This Town Out': Stokely Carmichael, Black Power, and the March against Fear," 2016, National Archives, https://rediscovering-black-history.blogs.archives.gov/2016/06/07/turn-this-town-out-stokely-carmichael-black-power-and-the-march-against-fear/ (accessed on April 1, 2019).
27. Bass and Devries, "John Lewis Interview," 60.
28. Ivanhoe Donaldson, "A Review on the Direction of SNCC—Past and Future," 1966, Veterans of the Civil Rights Movement, https://www.crmvet.org/docs/

660531_sncc_ivanhoe.pdf (accessed March 29, 2019).
29. Donaldson, "Review on the Direction of SNCC," 5.
30. SNCC Atlanta Project, "Basis of Black Power," 1966, Veterans of the Civil Rights Movement, https://www.crmvet.org/docs/blackpwr.htm (accessed February 27, 2019).
31. Clayborne Carson, *In the Struggle: SNCC and the Black Awakening of the 1960s* (Cambridge: Harvard University Press, 1995), 240.
32. Bill Ware, "Some Comments from the Staff Meeting and Why White People Should Be Excluded from the Meeting," 1966, Veterans of the Civil Rights Movement, https://www.crmvet.org/docs/660000_sncc_bp_whites.pdf (accessed March 20, 2019).
33. Jack Nelson, "SNCC Focuses Mood of Negro Rebellion," *Los Angeles Times* (1923-1995), 1967.
34. "SNCC Violent, Carmichael Says," 1967, *The Washington Post, Times Herald* (1959-1973), February 18, 1.
35. Stokely Carmichael, "What We Want," 1966, Veterans of the Civil Rights Movement, https://www.crmvet.org/info/stokely1.pdf (accessed April 1, 2019).
36. Carmichael, "What We Want," 7.
37. Stokely Carmichael, "Power and Racism," Veterans of the Civil Rights Movement, https://www.crmvet.org/info/stokely_p-r.pdf (accessed on April 1, 2019).
38. Stokely Carmichael, "Watts Speech," 1966, Veterans of the Civil Rights Movement, https://www.crmvet.org/info/661126_sncc_bp_watts.pdf (accessed March 27, 2019).
39. Stokely Carmichael, "Speech at the University of Puerto Rico," 1967, Veterans of the Civil Rights Movement, https://www.crmvet.org/docs/670125_sncc_speech.pdf (accessed March 27, 2019).
40. Carmichael, "Speech at the University of Puerto Rico," 2.
41. Robert Maynard, "SNCC without Carmichael Is Faltering," *The Washington Post, Times Herald* (1959-1973), September 20, 1968, 2.
42. James Forman, "The New SNCC," 1968, Veterans of the Civil Rights Movement, https://www.crmvet.org/docs/6807_sncc_newsncc.pdf (accessed March 29, 2019).
43. Femi Lewis, "The Student Nonviolent Coordinating Committee's Role in Civil Rights," 2018, Thought Co., https://www.thoughtco.com/student-nonviolent-coordinating-committee-45358 (accessed April 1, 2019).

7. The Color of Culture: The Black Power Movement and American Popular Culture

GIA THEOCHARIDIS

Introduction: Setting the Cultural Stage

You better watch out, you better not cry, you better not pout, I'm tellin' you why. Soul Santa is comin' to town. Christmas, 1968, in Chicago's South Side was wrapped in red, green, and gold. Boys, girls, and adults of all ages received gifts straight from Ghana from Soul Santa himself. The city's predominately black population joyously partook in Operation Breadbasket's "Black Christmas" celebration for the first time with presents, songs, and stories.[1] It was an event surrounded by black pride and unity, a darkening of the whitewashed holiday that enriched the African American community with inclusion and appreciation. Fast forward four months, and black Americans rejoiced together for the resurrection of Jesus Christ on Easter Sunday. The biblical prophet brought symbols of renewal and peace, a figure who adorned black skin. People celebrated "Black Easter" as a time of the renewal for the black community, as the white community celebrated Easter as the renewal of spring.[2] When December came around again, another sort of black Christmas would be celebrated with gifts and joy that allowed African acknowledgments to find their place in America's holiday calendar. Kwanzaa was a holiday that connected African Americans to their heritage, one that celebrated bountiful harvests and the hard work of the black community.

While various new celebrations commenced, musicians were hard at work authoring a new black narrative in the American arts and inspiring fellow members of their community to create in the same vein. Song lyrics began to bellow out politicized, soulful tunes of yearning for cultural acknowledgment, when they had previously emphasized more trivial topics such as romance. Record companies supported these up-and-coming black artists through efforts to produce their music and raise their reputations as performers. The nation would come to listen to new styles of music created entirely from the black journey to discover a unique identity. The lyrics would emulate the power and passion of the freedom struggle, the most well-known being soul and Motown. Black musicians encouraged the widespread appreciation of black culture and even reintegrated some lost genres like jazz that had been labeled white without acknowledging black influences. Music's rhythm emulated the frustrations of social contradictions of the 1960s, and its words hinted at political connotations. Emotional, politicized music was playing to the rhythm of celebrations while the fight for cultural discovery raged on.

This frenzy of black integration and separation in American popular culture was awakened by the actions of the Black Power movement. Black Power, which began in the late 1960s, advocated for universal black pride and celebration. It allowed black Americans to unite for the appreciation of an ancestry that was shared in their own history, separate from the dominant white narrative.[3] To achieve the creation of this new narrative, advocates created separate forms of music along with a new holiday exclusively for black Americans. However, the movement also made attempts to make white-dominated popular culture more inclusive for black Americans with initiatives like Soul Santa, Black Jesus, and the reclaiming of black-originated music genres.

Due to its stereotypical militant nature and the presence of the Black Panther Party, Black Power is often seen by history as nothing more than a coup against traditional white American society, culture, and politics – as an invasion rather than an integration. But the movement was more complex when it came to the formation of its desired cultural narrative. Advocates and pioneers of Black Power worked tirelessly together to alter white America's view of aspects of popular culture, such as holidays and music, without much, if any, violence. Only recently have scholars and historians begun to rethink Black Power in the positive light of cultural discovery and kind ambitions rather than the threat of brute force.[4] Through the examination of written sources such as newspapers and magazines accompanied by the analysis of music records and lyrics, this essay will expand the exploration of how Black Power shaped cultural reforms between whites and blacks in the late 1960s. Focusing on the realms of music and holidays, it will explore how the movement's inspiration managed to make "white" mainstream popular culture more accommodating and inclusive for black Americans while also helping blacks create a separate, unique cultural identity.

The Black American Revolution: The Rise of Black Power and the Search for an Identity

The phrase "Black Power" first appeared in the public eye in Richard Wright's 1954 book, *Black Power*. In this book, Wright wrote about his correspondence with Ghanaian prime minister Kwame Nkrumah and other African leaders and highlighted their discussions about what needed to be done in America to make its society more suitable for black Americans.[5] Although the title first appeared more than a decade before the movement gained popularity, it in many ways predicted what would occur in the United States. However, the introduction of "Black Power" as it was known in the late 1960s was first introduced at a march by a civil rights activist named Willie Ricks in March 1966.[6] It would become a forceful social, political, and especially cultural phenomenon that worked to find a place for black Americans in a white society. But it also had ambitions to create a separate sort of American identity for blacks that connected them to their African ancestry and roots, something that erased white influence completely from the picture. It would become a movement driven by opposing forces of integration and a new form of segregation.

The Black Power movement was the product of the civil rights struggles of the early 1960s. Its motives, however, moved far beyond vying for basic political rights, such as the right to vote without discrimination and the right to use shared public facilities with the white population. By August 6, 1965, those rights had been won and black Americans had gained the basic framework of equality of citizenship. Nevertheless, they also began to confront the reality that they were still, in several ways, second-class citizens in a society where whiteness reigned supreme. The black population was in a situation of what writer Robert Allen called *domestic colonialism*, in which it was regulated by a dominant entity and restrained from living under independent terms.[7] Before the rise of the Black Power movement, African Americans essentially lived by the social and cultural standards of the white population.

Both groups celebrated holidays in similar ways, and the forms of music they listened to were mostly uniform. Dimensions of popular culture, such as holidays and music, often featured central iconic celebrities who were white or, if not white, were at least geared towards a white audience. This submissive expectation was challenged by the Black Power movement and by those black Americans who wanted to start seeing things in a different light and color.

The cultural works of Black Power activists involved conjoining ideals of both integration and separation while increasingly exhibiting the need for an independent black identity. They called upon other black artists, activists, and citizens to join the new revolution. Mostly driven by politics, activist Stokely Carmichael had defined the movement as "the ability of black people to politically get together and organize themselves so that they can speak from a position of strength rather than a position of weakness."[8] Despite the movement having a strong political foundation, it also resulted in many social reforms, including the redefining of popular culture. Popular culture, in fact, was an integral part of making politics during the era of the black freedom struggle because activists challenged the norm with the increasing presence of black participation and reform.[9] The Black Power movement gave blacks a new sense of desire for more involvement and inclusion in popular culture as well as more representation. Artists and activists alike would use their work to try to spread this cultural identity all around America, and even the world.

Seizing the Time: Black Power and Music

American music in the days before Black Power carried a much lighter tone and rhythm than the bubbly doo-wop music commonly associated with the 1950s and early 1960s. The music that dominated the industry emphasized high-spirited melodies and romantic lyrics. Naturally, most of the famous artists were white. Music was not generally political or controversial, and many songs sounded alike, with surrounding themes of romantic love or young living. But even records performed by black artists such as the Supremes or the Jackson 5 began as typical for the time period's style of music: light-hearted and easy to comprehend. As the force of Black Power gained momentum, however, what was once breezy pop music morphed into upbeat groovy ballads with heavier messages of black pride and a demand for equality. Black musicians developed new genres of music in their efforts to create a black musical repertoire with striking political messages. Simultaneously, Black Power musicians and supporters attempted to integrate the music industry in nature and sound while reclaiming styles that had been founded by blacks but credited to whites. Black Power moved music in new directions concerning both white and black musicians, meshing their melodies but also tearing them into separate song.[10]

The quest for the integration of music during the Black Power era was exhibited in the formation of bands such as Sly and the Family Stone. Formed in 1967, this racially integrated band was made up of two women and five men, two of whom were white, but all were avid advocates for racial equality. The group performed blended music of flower-child rock and soul, especially when soul music was losing white audiences.[11] Sly and the Family Stone wrote and performed their own songs on the war, drugs, and – mostly – racial issues in which they expressed their discontent with the segregated nature of America. The group's most popular song, "Everyday People," serves as an anthem that declares that "we got to live together" and that it "makes no difference what group I'm in."[12] The song demonstrates the group's typical style while conveying a powerful message. "Groovy" music introduced a new form of rhythm in the 1960s with blends of rock and soul notes along with high-pitched lyrics. "Everyday People" even repeats that "there is a yellow one that won't accept the black one, that won't accept the red one that won't accept the white one. And so on and so on," which is a lyric that indicates that racism will always exist, but people must learn to move past it to live together in peace.[13] The group advocated for more racial unity despite the continuing presence of racism in America.

Sly and the Family Stone's other songs, like "We Love All" and "Harmony," also conveyed the message that people of all races needed to unite. Other songs by the band, however, were more controversial in nature, especially "Don't Call Me a Nigger, Whitey." This is a song that does exactly what the title says, but even in reverse. Sung by white and black people together, the only two lyrics in the song are "don't call me nigger, whitey" and "don't call me whitey, nigger" against a psychedelic, surreal synthesizer type of tune, almost one that exhibits the blending of rock and soul sounds.[14] Again, this is a song with uncomfortable language, but it demonstrates that the band believed solidarity must exist between races and that acceptance of abstaining from offensive slurs for each other was required. Sly and the Family Stone was a group that, through its music, displayed the desire for racial integration that existed even during the Black Power era. Through the band members' skin colors, powerful lyrics, and integrated sounds of white and black music, the group conveyed the call for racial pride and appreciation on both ends of the color spectrum.

Rock artist Jimi Hendrix is a perfect example of the Black Power initiative of reclaiming music styles that were stolen by white artists from their black counterparts. Hendrix was a rock 'n' roll artist who came to be known as the "Black Elvis" by some like Michael Lydon.[15] Rock music, like jazz music, had roots in black American sounds. Jazz lyrics were slow and carried much resemblance to those of African slave songs of earlier days passed down by their ancestors, often mirroring their struggles through their cries for freedom.[16] Rock music, however, took a more forceful directive towards the demand for racial justice with its hard notes and guitar licks that were extremely popular in white America. The genre was taken over by whites with the rise of Elvis, and even Hendrix's nickname, "Black Elvis," demonstrated how that artificial ownership remained. Hendrix gained the name because his music carried the classical rock 'n' roll tone with smooth tunes and steady rhythm. He also had similar popular stage movements as Elvis. According to journalist Michael Lydon, "he played flicking his gleaming white Gibson between his legs and propelling it out with his groin and a nimble grind of his hips," movements that were considered indecent for the 1960s.[17] Although Hendrix's lyrics were not largely controversial like other artists, he reclaimed rock 'n' roll for black Americans through his mirroring performance of one of the most popular rock stars of white America.

Music made during the Black Power era not only attempted to integrate and reclaim white styles but also helped create new genres of music that were dedicated and credited exclusively to black Americans. Traditional rock and jazz never left the musical scene, but a new form of music was created through newfound Black Power: soul. Soul music was a result of the stereotypical lower-class African American jazz singer rejecting middle-class American culture.[18] "Soul" itself has been defined as "an attempt to strike at the heart of the ethic of success and mobility," and black musicians followed through with its definition.[19] Once confined by socioeconomic status, poor and working-class black American musicians were becoming increasingly empowered by their origins and conveyed their feelings in their music. Rhythms that were considered "soul" were much more upbeat and livelier, unlike the usual slow laments of jazz, and thus conveyed messages of encouragement. However, in some songs, there remained some smooth elements of jazz, like the easygoing saxophone tunes that are often associated with the genre. Black Power focused on helping and encouraging black Americans of all social classes and statuses to engage in artistic and social life, in contrast to a white society that typically kept the activists of social classes separate and distinct. Soul music gave lower-class blacks a place in music that allowed them to exhibit pride for their lifestyles. Black Pride was a central message of the rhythms and lyrics of soul music, which were echoed by the Black Power movement.

Another example of Black Power segregating music was exhibited in the classic "Detroit Sound" of Motown. The Motown style gained its name through its birth at the Motown Record Studio in Detroit, Michigan. Founded by Berry Gordy, Motown Records was, as Robb Baker explained at the time, "formed to make sure Negro artists had the chance."[20] Many of America's most iconic black performers got their start at Motown Records, including Marvin Gaye, the Supremes, the Jackson 5, and Stevie Wonder. The sound that was produced at the Detroit studio became its own genre, a style that blended church gospel, smooth jazz, and street corner symphony.[21] "Motown" was short for Motortown, the name given to Detroit because of its booming automobile production industry.[22] This new genre of music was a style unlike anything that ever rang out of America's radios during the times of rock, pop, and bee-bop music. Black artists combined their soulful voices with emotional lyrics, which gave a unique identity to the new music style. Marvin Gaye began his career at Motown Records and created hits such as "What's Going On?" Produced in 1971 in response to the Vietnam War, the song cries, "Brother, brother, there's far too many of you dyin'" and "Father, father, we don't need to escalate" because "war is not the answer."[23] His album of the same name contained other songs confronting racial issues and violence. Gaye's take on Motown style is clear in this powerful political song through his voice of soul and feeling. The overall nature of his music was confrontational towards highlighted issues of the 1960s, and even the 1970s tied in with the new style of the Motown machine. Motown was a genre created by blacks for blacks, but it was given to all of America. It was a genre that had soul and power, two central forces of Black Power that were evident in its words and sounds.

Lyrics that were once tragic in jazz increasingly became belting words of pride and optimism along with powerful messages of resistance during the Black Power era. Songs conveyed phrases that made their listeners feel positive about being black during a time when they were shamed by white musicians. James Brown's song "Say It Loud—I'm Black and I'm Proud," for example, echoed a central theme of the Black Power movement. Produced in 1968, Brown's song was full of groovy rhythms and soulful feelings with loud, high-spirited declarations. It consisted of lyrics like "some people say we got a lot of malice; some say it's a lotta nerve. But I say we won't quit movin' until we get what we deserve" in response to the civil rights movement, saying that the fight for equality will never end.[24] The song repeats the phrase "I'm Black and I'm Proud" several times, which turned into a mantra for all black Americans to recite. A notable feature of the song was the fact that the cheers of "I'm black and I'm proud" were belted out by children. A central critique during the Black Power movement was the lack of African American education lessons in school systems of America. Using children to declare that they were proud to be black demonstrated to young black Americans that they too could be proud. Brown was aiming to make other Americans feel proud to be black, which was a motive of many other musicians of the Black Power era. Singers who supported the movement wanted to recruit other blacks to feel the same sense of empowerment they did from songs of resistance, pride, and unity.

The influential Black Panther Party of the late 1960s also had a significant impact on black American music. Although the party was made up of the most forceful political activists and gained a negative reputation for its militancy, it used its force to influence musical artists like Elaine Brown. The African American singer would write the national anthem of the Black Panthers, titled "The Meeting," in 1969. It first appeared in her album *Seize the Time*, an album that she wrote all on her own that included other songs such as "And All Stood By" and "The End of Silence."[25] "The Meeting" was a song that was a mixture of jazzy lamentation but soulful hopefulness that conveyed a message that black Americans would persevere and that they must seize their time to succeed through its strife by staying strong. "Man, am I coming through," Brown repeatedly declared while telling the story of a black man talking of his past oppression, indicating that she and others too will survive the same kind of oppression.[26] After she produced *Seize the Time*, Brown remained an active member of the Black Panther Party and eventually served as minister of information in the party's Central Committee. The Black Panther Party formed a funk house band called the Lumpen, which performed popular black music of the time to convey the party's goals through performance.[27] The band was considered "revolutionary" to the party, and their concerts were full of dancing and tunes of Black Power, radicalism, and soul.[28]

The Black Power era shaped the integration and reclaiming of music genres for Americans of all races, created new black styles of music for black Americans to pride themselves on, inspired artists to write music exhibiting black optimism, and led to the formation of a band for its central party. Bands and music lyrics alike became more united while also a little bit separated from each other. However, the harmonies worked in conjunction to create a new music industry for all of America. The Black Power movement's messages of black pride and unity uplifted the tunes of jazz and gave black American music a name that separated it from "white" music. Soul became the center of black music in America, and it was an example of how Black Power aimed for segregation from white popular culture, which was also exhibited through the uniqueness of Motown music. While accepting some white alliances into the groove, the black population seized its time, took new ownership of soul and Motown while reclaiming rock 'n' roll, making each funky melody jive to its own beat.

Happy Christmas, Merry Kwanzaa: Black Power and Holidays

The late 1960s was a time filled of holiday joy and change for the black community. Black Power was in its prime and shifted its influence in altering American holidays with motives of integration and segregation alike. Preexisting holidays that were dominated by white culture and influence, such as Christmas and Easter, turned into targets for the new integration initiatives in order to make them more inclusive and accommodating for black Americans. In efforts to make white holidays multicolored, black activists hosted Christmas and Easter celebrations that they dedicated to the black community. These were the beginnings of surrounding the meanings of these holidays around black influences and participation. However, integration was not the central motive of the Black Power holiday projects. The movement aided in the founding of an entirely new holiday exclusively for Americans of African descent to celebrate. Holidays for Black Power activists were another gateway into gaining a larger sense of black pride and appreciation in America through nationwide celebration of well-known events by all skin colors.

In November 1968, Operation Breadbasket, sponsored by the Southern Christian Leadership Conference (SCLC), hosted its first "Black Christmas" celebration in South Side Chicago. Besides the group's main goal of improving the living conditions of black communities around America, "Black Christmas" was led by Operation Breadbasket's director, the Reverend Jesse Jackson, who called on his fellow black Americans to boycott white merchants during their holiday shopping to protest what he called the "exploitation of Christmas" by the white population.[29] The celebration was also meant to shift the gratitude given to white figures like Santa Claus and instead give it to African American adults who worked hard to provide during the costly holiday season.[30] Santa was reinvented by "Black Christmas" and took on the name "Soul Santa," who came from Africa rather than the North Pole carrying candy and presents for all black Americans, regardless of social class, in a "soul power" sack.[31] He, of course, had black skin. Instead of red, white, and green, "Black Christmas" wrapped its joyous occasion in red, gold, and green to represent Ghana. Christmas was made to be in celebration of Africa but also retained the traditional aspects of the Americanized holiday.

Reverend Jackson wished to generate new perspectives on Christmas that were not so much anti-white as pro-black. He proclaimed that "the spirit of Christmas was born of God's ultimate act of giving. ... His example of love challenges us to promote the well-being of others to share our abundance with the less fortunate in jails, hospitals, and other institutions."[32] "Black Christmas" was unique not only because it promoted inclusion for African Americans but also because it asked people to give to those who were less fortunate than them. It gave a much more charitable rather than commercialized aspect of Christmas. This was an initiative that was incredibly meaningful within black communities that often had to deal with rampant poverty and crime, like in inner-city Chicago. The holiday's commercialism often promoted by white communities was eliminated by "Black Christmas" and gave it the new perspectives of black identity and cultural values that Reverend Jackson sought to achieve for the good of the communities he helped through Operation Breadbasket. The organization promoted a message of "dreaming of a *Black Christmas* ... *not* like the ones I used to know," rather than "I'm dreaming of a *white Christmas. Just* like the ones I used to know."

Operation Breadbasket and SCLC aimed to make Easter a more inclusive holiday for black Americans as well. "Black Easter" was first celebrated in 1969 during an event and play honoring Dr. Martin Luther King Jr. after the first anniversary of his death.[33] Like Black Christmas, "Black Easter" aimed to focus on the black influences of beauty, love, and productivity rather than the traditional focus on the white population. Jesus Christ was portrayed as a man with black skin, as it had been speculated for centuries that he was indeed black, on a day that honored renewal and peace. White Americans often celebrated Easter as a renewal of spring, but "Black Easter" celebrated the day as renewal of the black community.[34] In the words of Reverend Jackson, "Black Easter will be an expression of determination on the part of the black people to offer themselves in renewal and re-education, which marks the redemptive opening of new life for the black and the poor."[35] Jackson also saw "Black Easter" as an opportunity to promote a new sense of imagery and belonging in the black population and wanted to pass the message "I am somebody, we are somebody."[36] Easter Sunday for the black American population would come to represent both pride and peace within each person's personal life and their community as one body.

In the search of a separate black cultural identity, Black Power activists went beyond the efforts of activists like Jesse Jackson to help establish a new holiday that solely celebrated black culture: Kwanzaa. *Kwanzaa* is a Swahili term that means "first fruits," and it was a holiday founded to celebrate bountiful harvests of crops in Africa with gifts, songs, thanksgiving, feasts, and dances.[37] The holiday was first celebrated from December 26 to January 1, 1966. Kwanzaa was created by Maulana Karenga, who was an active advocate for the Black Power movement in the 1960s and 1970s.[38] Karenga promoted the creation of Kwanzaa for the purpose of advancing the creation of an entirely new black lifestyle in America.[39] He declared that the holiday would value seven principles that involved maintaining unity, respect-

The Color of Culture | 115

ing families, and defining and speaking for oneself as an African American. Kwanzaa was a happy, colorful holiday that was plentiful in celebration, gifts, and love.

Kwanzaa took inspiration from similar celebrations in Africa. Promoting the celebration of the holiday and its explicit meanings was one method used by Black Power activists to connect African Americans to their heritage and ancestry in the far-off continent where their ancestors were taken from and brought to America as slaves. It gave headway to the promotion of "pan-Africanism," an idea which means to work towards solidarity between native people and descendants of Africa. It was a rather optimistic holiday that quickly became a part of mainstream American popular culture and consumer culture. Corporate America did not hesitate to endorse the holiday to sell mass-produced goods and decorations for the events of the holiday, which demonstrated the level of influence of the Black Power movement.[40] The movement was able to break into corporate America and in turn gained publicity for its goals through companies promoting its creation of a holiday.[41] However, Kwanzaa's focus on gratitude and family was seen as a way of "de-whiting or taking commercialism out of [the] time of year," as Alfred Sharpton said after a Kwanzaa celebration he had hosted for black children.[42] It was a powerful method to create a separate black culture identity that stood in contrast to the overly commercialized dominant white holiday traditions. Not only did Kwanzaa aid in the formation of a separate black cultural identity in America, it also helped spread the messages of the Black Power movement that included brotherhood, love, peace, and unity.

Holidays, as promoted by black activists, had more effects than just integrating and segregating American popular culture. They were supposed to be times of celebration of the black community and everything that it stood for. Holidays like Christmas, Easter, and Kwanzaa had influences on aiding the less fortunate and being grateful for gifts. People of all ages and backgrounds would come together to give to the black community and share the newfound senses of pride and unity. The loving and accepting nature of these holidays by the black community had effects on healing ex and current black drug addicts during the season. The "Soul Saving Station" aired programs during the Christmas and Kwanzaa season that were aimed at bringing people closer to God, as doing drugs was considered "being away from God."[43]

Black people, especially those ravaged by tragedy, felt as if the holiday seasons could bring healing through faith and love that could be felt by every member of the community.

Messages of positivity and acceptance drove the black community into finding a new identity for themselves that was free of white commercialism and full of revival for a once-oppressed people. Black Jesus and Soul Santa showed the community that their efforts towards making the holiday seasons were not forgotten. Kwanzaa, on its own, dedicated appreciation and celebration for black Americans with love straight from Africa. The prideful joy of the Black Power movement took the holidays to a new level. The Black Power movement directly affected the nature of holidays in America by using its branch organizations which were led by the movement's activists and supporters that worked together to achieve its contrasting goals of integration and separation. Inclusiveness, yet exclusiveness, was discovered for the black American population through holidays like Kwanzaa and Black Christmas and Easter celebrations. Appreciation and gratitude for the laborious work of black Americans was displayed during these holidays, and it created a larger sense of unity within the community, which is exactly what the Black Power movement had been advocating for since its beginnings.

Conclusion: Painting Popular Culture a Different Color

The Black Power movement and its allies dealt with the cultural tensions in America in the heated days of the civil rights movement by working to ease them for both whites and blacks. Aspects of American popular culture, such as music and holidays, were integrated for the sense of making "white" culture more accommodating and inclusive for black Americans while also segregated to help create a separate, unique cultural identity for the black community. Music became much more upbeat with more striking lyrics and messages, which were sung by black and white artists alike, at times together. Genres of music that were heavily influenced by black people that were claimed by the whites as their own were recaptured into the black identity. Removing aspects of whiteness such as commercialism in holidays allowed for holidays like Kwanzaa to promote the pride and love of blackness, while Black Easter and Christmas paid tribute to the hard-working nature of the black community.

A central motif of Black Power was to ignite a new sense of black acceptance and pride for Americans. The incorporation of this sense of black positivity into popular culture allowed for the influence of new ideals to greatly increase. America would come to recognize black greatness through the community's new additions and involvements in popular culture. The music flowing through the radios would carry the voices of black and white musicians in unison against the groove of soul while a black guitarist's riffs would wail. Motown would hit cities across America while people lit the candles of Kwanzaa. Christmas cheer would be passed between black families with gifts of thanks and candy from Soul Santa. The next generation would come to see Black Power in holiday celebrations and hear it in the notes of their old-time Motown records they found in the attic. Black Power would follow through America's history and forever belt the message, "Say it loud–I'm black and I'm proud!!"

Notes

1. "I'm Dreaming of a Black Christmas," *Ebony*, November 1969, 115.
2. "... And a Black Easter," *Ebony*, November 1969, 119.
3. Robert L. Allen, *A Guide to Black Power in America: A History Analysis* (London: Gollancz, 1970), 7.
4. Several writers have explored the nonviolent ways that the Black Power movement forced change into popular culture, despite popular belief that the movement was always militant. See: Richard Iton, *In Search of the Black Fantastic: Politics and Popular Culture in the Post-Civil Rights Era* (New York: Oxford University Press, 2010); Allen, *A Guide to Black Power in America*; William L. Van Deburg, *New Day in Babylon: The Black Power Movement and American Culture, 1965–1975* (Chicago: University of Chicago Press, 1992).
5. Judson Jeffries, *Black Power in the Belly of the Beast* (Urbana: University of Illinois, 2006), 2–3.
6. Jeffries, *Black Power in the Belly of the Beast*, 6.
7. Allen, *A Guide to Black Power in America*, 2.
8. Joyce Ladner, "What 'Black Power' Means to Negros in Mississippi," *Transaction*, 1967, 7–15.
9. Iton, *In Search of the Black Fantastic*, 8.

10. Several writers have acknowledged the nature of music before and after the start of the Black Power era. See: Mark Anthony Neal, *Soul Babies: Black Popular Culture and the Post-Soul Aesthetic* (New York: Routledge, 2002); Van Deburg, *New Day in Babylon*; Monique Guillory and Richard Green, *Soul: Black Power, Politics, and Pleasure* (New York: New York University Press, 1998).
11. Barbara Campbell, "Pop: Sly Stone is Together," *New York Times*, February 1, 1970, D35.
12. Sly and the Family Stone, "Everyday People–Stand!," 1969, YouTube, https://www.youtube.com/watch?v=YUUhDoCx8zc (accessed April 14, 2019).
13. Sly and the Family Stone, "Everyday People–Stand!," 1969.
14. Sly and the Family Stone, "Don't Call Me a Nigger, Whitey–Stand!," 1969, YouTube, https://www.youtube.com/watch?v=0_VfGVKzcfs (accessed April 13, 2019).
15. Michael Lydon, "The Black Elvis?," *New York Times*, February 25, 1968, D19.
16. Archie Shepp, "Black Power and Black Jazz," *New York Times*, November 26, 1967, J1.
17. Lydon, "The Black Elvis?," D19.
18. Guillory and Green, *Soul: Black Power, Politics, and Pleasure*, 34.
19. Berger Bennet, "Black Culture: Lower Class Result or Ethnic Creation?," *Soul*, ed. Lee Rainwater (Chicago: Aldine, 1970).
20. Robb Baker, "It Was a 'Rock-Em, Sock-Em' Week-End," *Chicago Tribune*, March 10, 1968, A4.
21. "The Sound that Changed America," *Motown Sound*, Motown Museum, Detroit, Michigan, https://www.motownmuseum.org/motown-sound/the-artists/ (accessed March 15, 2019).
22. Pete Johnson, "The Man the Motown Sound Revolves Around," *Los Angeles Times*, August 18, 1968, C1.
23. Marvin Gaye, "What's Going On?," *What's Going On?*, 1971, YouTube, https://www.youtube.com/watch?v=H-kA3UtBj4M (accessed April 14, 2019).
24. James Brown, "Say It Loud–I'm Black and I'm Proud," *Say It Loud–I'm Black and I'm Proud*, 1968, YouTube, https://www.youtube.com/watch?v=9bJA6W9CqvE (accessed April 16, 2019).
25. Joel Skidmore, "Panther's Turbulent Career," *Sun Reporter*, December 25, 1971, 12.
26. Elaine Brown, "The Meeting," *Seize the Time*, 1969, YouTube, https://www.youtube.com/watch?v=4JsDMwUE4mI (accessed April 16, 2019).
27. Rickey Vincent and Boots Riley, *Party Music: The Inside Story of the Black Panthers Band and How Black Power Transformed Soul Music* (Chicago: Chicago Review Press, 2013), 5.
28. Vincent and Riley, *Party Music*, 4.
29. "Jackson Kicks Off 2d 'Black Christmas,'" *Chicago Tribune*, November 29, 1969, A9.
30. "Jackson Kicks Off 2d 'Black Christmas,'" A9.
31. "I'm Dreaming of a Black Christmas," 115.
32. "I'm Dreaming of a Black Christmas," 118.
33. "Passion Play to Mark King's Death," *Chicago Daily*, March 1, 1969, 1.
34. "... And a Black Easter," 119.
35. Jesse Jackson, "'Country Preacher' on the Case," *Chicago Daily Defender*, March 28, 1970, 1.

36. "... And a Black Easter," 119.
37. Angela Terrell, "Reaping the Fruits of Kwanzaa," *The Washington Post, Times Herald*, December 19, 1972, B3.
38. A. N., "Kwanzaa: Creating a Black Value System," *Sun Reporter*, December 30, 1972, 9.
39. A. N., "Kwanzaa: Creating a Black Value System," *Sun Reporter*, December 30, 1972, 9.
40. Keith A. Mayes, *Kwanzaa: Black Power and the Making of the African-American Holiday Tradition* (New York: Routledge, 2009), xx.
41. Mayes, *Kwanzaa*, xxi.
42. Charlayne Hunter, "Spirit of Kwanza: A Time of Giving," *New York Times*, December 24, 1971, 28.
43. "Love and Faith a Cure for Some Addicts," *Bay State Banner*, December 30, 1971, 6.

8. Black Is Beautiful: Mirroring the Media

CLAIRE KO

> My daughter doesn't know about life before black became beautiful, when black was the color of a shoe, or the night, but never the color of a person. In those days, if someone called you "black," you didn't stick your fist in the air, you stuck it in their face.
>
> – Patrice Gaines-Carter[1]

A sea of pale faces and pin-straight hair plastered both white and black magazines throughout the 1960s. That image infiltrated the minds of many black women attempting to assimilate themselves within a white-dominated society. Skin-bleaching and hair-straightening product advertisements embedded themselves within black media and served as a model of what black women should strive to look like. The supposedly superior beauty ideal of white womanhood was perpetuated in popular media across the United States, which shamed women who did not parade fair skin and unkinked hair, even during an era of unprecedented activism and legislation for black civil rights. "Radical" and "militant" black activists, however, took the civil rights movement a step further and emphasized black racial pride as the focal point of their cause with the emergence of the Black Power movement.

The establishment of Black Power birthed a sub-movement known as "Black is Beautiful," in which black women embraced not only their African heritage but also the darker skin and kinky hair that came with it. The surge of racial pride within the African American community of the 1960s influenced many black women to reflect on how they digested the almost impossible white beauty standards that they saw in popular media, such as magazines and newspapers. As black nationalist activists created their own propaganda for the Black Power movement, they started to put down the harsh chemicals and headed toward a journey for liberation from Eurocentric cultural conformity.

Most historical accounts discuss the significance of this turn to Afrocentric pride by highlighting both individual and group efforts that rejected white societal norms throughout the 1960s, '70s, and '80s. This discussion emphasizes the political and societal stratification the black population faced but also the ways they utilized their appearance as an explicit form of activism and protest. Generally, scholars have connected economics, politics, and society to contribute to the widespread notion that the Black is Beautiful movement was an integral part of breaking away from cultural norms and redefining beauty for the African American community.[2]

This chapter will examine popular black media and its influence on beauty standards for black women. Investigating magazines and newspapers specifically geared toward a black female audience provides an image of what this audience thought an ideal black woman should look like. How were black women portrayed in black popular media prior to the emergence of the Black is Beautiful movement? How did popular black magazines and newspapers respond to the Black is Beautiful movement? How did activists and followers of the movement contribute to its message? Answering these questions will reveal how black women not only responded to beauty standards within popular media, but how they redefined it. Although popular media took longer to respond to the Black is Beautiful movement, its inclusion of a broader definition of black beauty showed that mainstream society adapted to what was considered "radical" and "militant."

Context

The Black is Beautiful movement arose at the height of the Black Power era, during the late 1960s and early 1970s. Black Power activists were the political actors in this movement that promoted the slogan Black is Beautiful. The movement encouraged black women to embrace their natural hair and helped redefine black beauty standards for the African American community. Part of the Black Power mission was to promote the ideal that black was beautiful and that black women should stop supporting white society's beauty standards. Several white companies such as Avon, Clairol, Perma-Strate, and Nadinola developed cosmetics particularly suited for black women to lighten their skin and straighten their hair.[3] Many African American corporations, such as Johnson Products and Supreme Beauty Products, were quick to adopt the movement's message and counter these white companies by producing beauty products that enhanced a black woman's features. The development of new products that encouraged natural black beauty for African American women allowed beauty to be defined in broader ways.

Since white society dictated what was considered "beautiful" during the 1960s and 1970s, many African Americans, as historian Obiagele Lake argues, "bought into the idea that thick lips, dark skin, and nappy hair [were] not beautiful."[4] However, black women expressed their desire for a more inclusive society through hairstyles and fashion during the 1960s. Natural hairstyles for black women, such as the afro, were as fashionable as they were political.[5] Many black women started to embrace afros as a form of self-expression and a political statement to fight against the white ideal. Black fashion shows celebrated "transgressive style politics" and were made popular by informal fashion magazines, which highlighted Afrocentric fashion designers.[6] Although outside of the mainstream media, the rise of black cultural fashion became another outward form of political expression of black nationalism.

The Black is Beautiful movement provided support for many black women to take a huge step toward liberation from the strict rules of white beauty. According to feminist sociologist Meeta Rani Jha, "if femininity is defined by the absence of blackness, then the role the Black is Beautiful movement played is one of the most significant anti-racist challenges to the dominant white beauty, destabilizing its cultural power."[7] The movement served as a catalyst for black women to change the course of societal norms and make themselves known for who they naturally were. It not only allowed black women to express themselves and demonstrate national pride but was also a political statement against the dominant white society that attempted to control other aspects of their lives, such as education, jobs, and presence in politics. Sociologist Margaret L. Hunter's article "If You're Light You're Alright" revealed the implications darker-skinned women faced in terms of education, personal income, and spousal status. According to her findings, "skin color modifie[d] outcomes and produce[d] advantages for the light skinned."[8] The acceptance of the Black is Beautiful movement by black women, whether through activism or the consumption of media, paved a way for the African American community to fight against white society's oppressive authority during the 1960s.

Whiter Skin and Straighter Hair

Popular black media, such as magazines and newspapers, served as an essential influence on fashion, beauty, and lifestyle for middle-class black women. *Ebony* magazine, *Jet* magazine, the *Chicago Daily Defender*, and the *Baltimore Afro-American* were just a few forms of media that the African American community regularly read. In the early 1960s, the images and advertisements that represented black women mainly showcased paler skin and straight hair. This depiction of black women pervaded the minds of average African American consumers and made them believe it was only acceptable to have white characteristics to fit into society. Many of the same advertisements that promoted skin lighteners and chemical hair straighteners appeared across different media forums. The strong influence that white society had on defining black beauty was especially apparent in the early 1960s, before the rise of the Black Power era, through the rhetoric and visual imagery that can be seen within popular black media.

Magazines such as *Ebony* and *Jet* advertised several different skin-bleaching companies and included many images of lighter-skinned black women. Nadinola Bleaching Cream, Dr. Fred Palmer's Double Strength Skin Whitener, Mercolized Wax Cream, and Posner's Skintona were a few skin-whitening brands that filled the pages. The rhetoric of these advertisements conveyed that having a lighter complexion would enhance the lives of black women. A popular Nadinola advertisement claimed that "life is more fun when your complexion is clear, bright, Nadinola-light!"[9] Another advertisement by Bleach and Glow Cream stated that its product would help "reveal a new, breath-taking, desirous, lighter, more creamy-looking complexion" for "no matter how dull or drab, coarse or dark your skin may be."[10] Advertisements consistently encouraged the same ideal that whiter skin was more attractive and were paired with lighter-skinned black women to serve as the model. Slogans such as "lighter, brighter skin is irresistible" also implied that men would only be attracted to paler women.[11]

Figure 1: Nadinola advertisement that promoted "life is more fun" when you use the bleaching cream. The advertisement featured a lighter-skin black woman smiling with a man next to her. The message of this advertisement was to show that having a lighter complexion would attract men and invoke happiness (Ebony, January 1960, 91).

It was rare to see a dark-skinned black woman in advertisements at all in the early 1960s, which furthered the notion that darker skin was not beautiful enough to be featured in mainstream media.

Black women worried not only about their skin complexion but also about the texture and appearance of their hair. Early editions of *Ebony* and *Jet* constantly advertised hair products that shamed kinky hair and promoted

Black Is Beautiful | 125

straighter, longer hair. An eXelento Hair Pomade advertisement asserted that its product's "first application [made] frizzy kinky hair look naturally longer – alive – radiant."[12] This explicit disapproval of kinky hair showcased the negative attitude society had toward black women's natural hair. Perma-Strate, a cold permanent cream hair straightener, was designed to remove "all the undesirable kink and too-tight curls to give soft, natural-looking straight hair for 3 months or longer."[13] Ironically, these advertisements marketed "natural-looking straight hair" when they were anything but natural for black women. There were no advertisements that promoted afros or kinky hair within the early editions of these magazines. The early 1960s did not represent black women with afros because it was considered abnormal to accept a hairstyle that differed from the ideal white standard.

TEEN-AGE TORTURE

Blemishes, blackheads, breakouts and pimples cause untold misery to millions of teen-agers. There's no need to be miserable. Active, foamy medication of Palmer's "SKIN SUCCESS" Soap combats skin germs that often spread infections and may cause blackheads and pimples. While "SKIN SUCCESS" Soap works to reveal a lovely complexion, it gives you effective deodorant protection, too.

More effective than greasy creams for pimples, blackheads and many skin eruptions.

For complexion success and date success use "SKIN SUCCESS" Bleach Cream after using "SKIN SUCCESS" Soap. Wakes up your complexion to clearer, fresher beauty. Don't just cover up — bleach your troubles away. "SKIN SUCCESS" Bleach Cream fades blackheads, freckles and dark sun spots as it smoothes out roughness and helps keep your skin soft and clear looking. Don't be embarrassed a day longer. Get new, improved Palmer's "SKIN SUCCESS" Bleach Cream. Now contains more ammoniated mercury, the active skin bleacher, than any leading brand. For a lovely attractive complexion ask for "SKIN SUCCESS".

PALMER'S "SKIN-SUCCESS" SOAP BLEACH CREAM

Figure 2: Palmer's "Skin-Success" advertisement that claimed "complexion success." To achieve a "lovely attractive complexion" meant achieving "success." This rhetoric led the audience to believe that if they had darker skin, it was considered "unsuccessful" and generally not accepted by the public (Ebony, January 1960, 73).

The African American community could not escape the images of whiter skin and straight hair even after putting down magazines. Skin-altering and hair-straightening advertisements were prevalent within prominent black newspapers as well, which reinforced the importance of achieving white standards for black women. Newspapers did not discuss beauty standards or advertise beauty products as frequently as magazines did, but advertisements for skin bleaches and hair straighteners still appeared. An advertisement in the *Chicago Daily Defender* for Palmer's "Skin-Success" Soap and Bleach Cream said, "Don't be embarrassed a day longer," and promised "complexion success" through its use of "more ammoniated mercury, the active skin bleacher."[14] In the *Baltimore Afro-American*, an advertisement for Perma-Strate asserted that it was the "one cream hair straightener preferred and recommended by such famous stars as Sarah Vaughan, Count Basie, and many others."[15] This advertisement appealed to the public by including prominent black celebrities that supposedly used this product, which also made the process of hair straightening desirable. The *Baltimore Afro-American* newspaper also promoted a product called Be-Gone Bleach Cream, which claimed that "smooth heavenly kissable skin doesn't just happen."[16] Its rhetoric implied that black women had to use this product to achieve "Georgia Peach Skin" and to be "delighted."[17] Newspapers were another way for white beauty standards to persist through the publication of beauty advertisements.

Expanding the Color Palette

Radical forms of media, which directly challenged the political, cultural, and racial status quo and made direct contributions to the Black is Beautiful movement, appeared as early as 1963. This media publicized the Black is Beautiful movement and spread the word about its mission not only to the African American community, but to the white community as well. Since this type of media completely went against what was socially acceptable within white society, it was considered "militant." Unlike popular black media, this "militant" media arose and contributed several images and symbols of black power throughout the sixties.

Kwame Brathwaite, a New York photographer, used his photography as a medium for activism. His portfolio consists of several images that "worked to disrupt media and produce positive images of African Americans."[18] The subjects of Brathwaite's photographs were mainly black women who proudly wore their afros and African-inspired garments and "who connected their natural hair to their politics."[19] According to law professor Richard Thompson Ford, hairstyles were "deeply significant expressions of racial pride and individual dignity, and thoughtless demands to alter one's hair [were] humiliating and stigmatizing."[20] Brathwaite used his photographs to counter this humiliation by capturing women's natural beauty as a form of protest.[21] Artistic expression, such as Brathwaite's photographs, was an effective way for the African American community to digest and accept the social changes that black activists wanted to enforce.

Brathwaite and his older brother, Elombe Brath, founded the African Jazz Arts Society and Studios (AJASS) in 1956, which "popularized the phrase 'Black is Beautiful' in the late '50s and early '60s."[22] AJASS organized "black cultural events, like jazz concerts at Club 845 in The Bronx ... where Brathwaite took photos of the jazz musicians and African dance performances," and was especially significant to the Black is Beautiful movement because of the "Naturally '62" fashion shows.[23] The models that participated in these fashion shows were known as the Grandassa Models. They were a group of black models that outwardly expressed a more "natural" look rather than one that fit the white ideal. The "Naturally" shows served to "make [African Americans] conscious of Africa and [their] heritage."[24] When the brothers first produced these "Naturally" shows, they were "laughed at by many people" because "very few black women were wearing their hair in ... the Afro style – kinky and unstraightened."[25] As a result, it was the women "with their 'exotic' African-inspired natural hairstyles, who garnered the most curiosity, criticism, and fanfare" since the debut of the "Naturally" shows.[26] Although these fashion shows were ridiculed at the beginning of their debut, AJASS continued to produce several more shows until the late 1970s.

The photographs and fashion shows produced by Kwame Brathwaite and his group, AJASS, were explicit examples of radical media that shaped the Black is Beautiful movement. The first "Naturally" show took place on January 28, 1962, at Harlem's Purple Manor and was advertised as "Naturally '62: The Original African Coiffure and Fashion Extravaganza Designed to Restore Our Racial Pride and Standards."[27] As previously mentioned, there were negative responses to these fashion shows by those who did not support the slogan Black is Beautiful. Kwame Brathwaite heard a man tell his brother, "You mean you're gonna put some nappy headed black bitches on stage to model?"[28]

Even with negative comments, AJASS and the Grandassa Models obtained a following of mainly black women that represented a variety of skin complexions, hair types, and personal backgrounds. Elombe Brathwaite stated that the purpose of these shows was to "persuade women of African descent to see the pride and beauty of wearing their hair in its natural state. In other words, to try and detour the trend that some black women [were] pursuing by imitating white women and becoming blondes, redheads."[29] Their goal to publicize the Black is Beautiful movement to a wide audience was successful. Kwame Brathwaite's photographs also allowed this audience to see a broader definition of black beauty. The subjects of his photographs were not light-skinned, straight-haired black women. Instead, they were black women who embraced different types of kinky hair and different shades of black skin. These forms of media expanded the term *beautiful* to mean something entirely different to mainstream media: they screamed that black was beautiful.

With the rise of the Black Power era, the slogan Black is Beautiful became popular amongst the African American community. The mid-1960s was the start of the Black Power era, when the political and racial slogan "Black Power" was first coined by Student Nonviolent Coordinating Committee (SNCC) organizers and spokespeople Stokely Carmichael and Willie Ricks.[30] Since then, many activists and followers outwardly expressed their support for black nationalism.

Popular black newspapers explicitly produced newspaper articles in the late 1960s and throughout the 1980s that addressed the Black is Beautiful movement, showcasing articles written by critics or supporters of the movement. Author Dr. Marcus H. Boulware declared that "the term 'black is beautiful' also [meant] 'black is proud' and also personal dignity" in 1969.[31]

Boulware's assertion shows that prominent figures discussed the significance of the slogan Black is Beautiful during the movement. Newspapers also gave voice to beauty experts, such as hair stylists and cosmeticians. In an article written in 1969 for the *Los Angeles Times*, writer Julie Byrne highlighted hair stylist Cleo Jackson's effort to "show how elegant the natural hairstyle [could] be" and also how cosmetician Barbara Walden "[applied] make-up, which she ... created to blend with and enhance dark skin" on her client.[32]

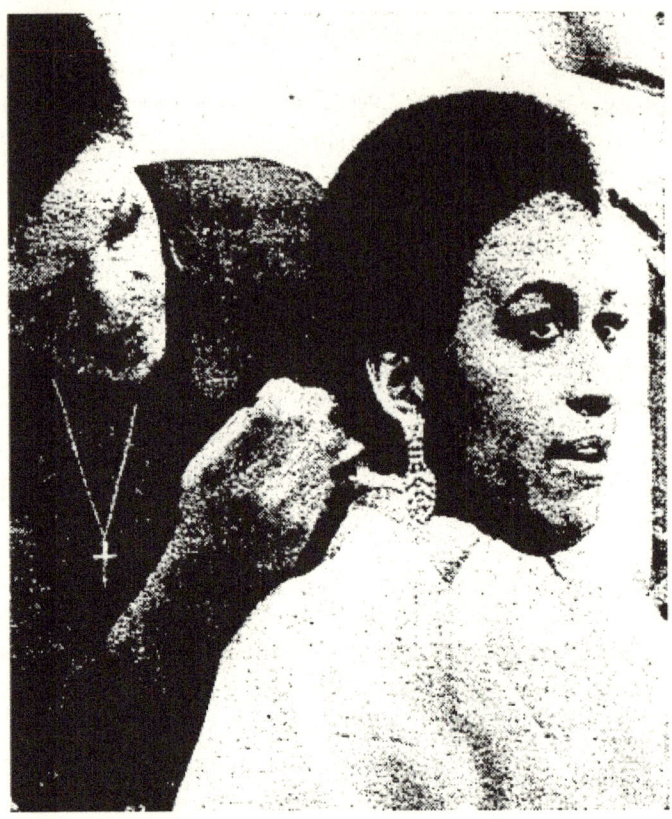

Figure 3: Hairstylist Cleo Jackson wearing an afro to show that it could be elegantly worn as a hairstyle for black women (Photo by Cal Montney, Los Angeles Times, March 4, 1969, H1).

A fascinating article written by Sandra Haggerty for the *Los Angeles Times* emphasized the viewpoint that not all supporters of the movement were "anti-white." According to Haggerty, the "illumination and glorification of blackness within ... society" was not "simultaneously an 'antiwhite thing.' ... It [was] simply viewing ... blackness as a positive rather than a negative aspect of" African Americans' being.[33] The Black is Beautiful movement made a strong impact on the African American community through its newspapers and was the subject of many conversations between scholars, activists, followers, and members of society.

Activists such as Kwame Brathwaite, Elombe Brath, and AJASS brought the Black is Beautiful movement to the forefront of society. Kwame's photographs highlighted black pride through the depiction of diverse and natural black models. The "Naturally '62" fashion shows were a publicly outward expression of black nationalism, which garnered a lot of attention from both black and white audiences. Due to the production of such "radical" media, the Black is Beautiful movement entered the arena of conversation. Scholars and writers discussed the significance of the movement in newspaper articles, which further shed light on its message of freedom from the white ideal. Media that contributed to the Black is Beautiful movement publicized the efforts of the movement's activists and expanded the color palette to include more shades than just white.

Becoming Naturally Beautiful

As the Black is Beautiful movement gained popularity, many Americans became familiar with the movement's message. Because of the rising popularity of these symbols of black power, such as afros and darker skin, popular media started to include images of these symbols into their advertisements. However, popular black media did not start to adopt that black was beautiful until the later 1960s and early 1970s.

Skin-lightening and hair-straightening advertisements were common even during the Black Power era. Although there were many activists that protested the white beauty standard, popular magazines did not adjust to representing darker skin on models until the 1970s. Lighter-skinned black women maintained their roles as models for the front cover of *Ebony* magazine all throughout the 1960s. The January 1970 front cover of *Ebony* was the first edition to showcase a darker-skinned model among the several issues that preceded it.[34] A significantly darker model did not appear on the front cover again until the May 1974 edition, which showcased actress Cicely Tyson as its model.[35] Even with the rise of Black Power imagery and symbols, it took popular black magazines longer to adjust to such radical ideas. However, although mainstream black media did not immediately respond to the Black is Beautiful movement during the mid-1960s, it started to include representations of darker-skinned women in the early 1970s.

Figure 4: Front cover of Ebony's September 1969 edition. This was the first cover of Ebony to feature an afro on a woman, which came approximately four years after the Black Power movement began. Its late debut proved that popular media slowly adjusted to the Black is Beautiful movement rather than immediately adopting it (Ebony, September 1969).

Similarly, it was not until September 1969 that *Ebony* magazine featured a black woman with an afro on its front cover.[36] After surveying the keyword *afros* in each January edition of *Ebony* throughout the 1960s, the first mention of afros was in the January 1969 edition. It appeared in an advertisement for Afro Sheen, which claimed that "it just keeps your Natural looking beautiful and healthy" and showed both a black man and black woman wearing an afro in its advertisement image.[37] This advertisement utilized the word *natural* in a much different way than hair-straightening advertisements, such as Perma-Strate, did. The word *natural* in the Afro Sheen advertisement was redefined to align itself with what black women considered to be "natural," rather than how white society defined it. Gold Medal, a wig company, stated what they considered to be "Now Styles" in its advertisement in the January 1974 edition of Ebony. Four out of the eight models wore afros, which showed that afros were considered an acceptable hairstyle for black women and men to wear at that point in time.[38] The acceptance of kinky hair through representation in magazines did not start to appear in the media until around the same time as darker skin did in the mid-1970s. As the Black is Beautiful movement strengthened throughout the late 1960s and 1970s, magazines became more willing to include women with afros in their images and advertisements.

The number and publication of skin-lightening and hair-straightening advertisements varied throughout the 1960s. Even with the emergence of the Black Power movement, these types of advertisements continued to persist into the 1970s. In the December 1969 edition of Ebony, a Perma-Strate advertisement declared that "every modern hair styling starts with straight hair!"[39] The persistence of advertisements that promoted culturally white ideals showed that popular media underwent a slow transition to embody the Black is Beautiful movement's message. However, the late 1960s and 1970s editions of Ebony did include more advertisements that enhanced the natural beauty of black women. For example, Murray's Superior Hair Dressing Pomade advertisement in the January 1974 edition of Ebony displayed a black man and woman with afros.[40] The advertisement did not in any way promote the straight-hair image that white society encouraged in the early 1960s. In the March 1970 edition of Ebony, an advertisement for Posner included several images of different hairstyles women could achieve with the product. Alongside straight hairstyles, there was an image of a black woman with an afro next to the "Posner Natural" product "for a beautiful Natural look."[41] Although the same skin-bleaching and hair-straightening products appeared in popular black media during the 1970s, there was an increase in more inclusive images and products that promoted natural black beauty as well.

The shift toward a more inclusive magazine occurred because their everyday consumers started to adopt new ideals that suggested black was beautiful. The emergence of darker-skinned models and products that enhanced afros were specifically curated for economic purposes. Due to the change in black pride and commodification of the Afro, both black and white companies "promoted products for use on Afros and depicted models with natural hair in their advertisements."[42] A large factor in transforming popular black media to include afros and dark skin was the market for beauty products and its effect on the economy.

Popular black media responded to the Black is Beautiful movement slowly because mainstream media did not want to conform to militant ideas. Mainstream media during the 1960s was designed to promote white beauty standards because that was what was considered "normal." These magazines were not meant to be revolutionary in nature and were created for the everyday, middle-class black consumer. What was once considered militant became the norm because of the movement's prevalence and support during this era. Magazines, like *Ebony*, were prime examples of how Black Power symbols slowly infiltrated the mainstream to push new beauty ideals.

Conclusion

Many of the participants in the Black Power era and the Black is Beautiful movement focused on entering the political arena to take a stand against white oppression. However, the movement was not just focused on obtaining political and economic equity. It also affected how black women were portrayed in media for the everyday consumer. Whether the readers of these black magazines and newspapers were activists or not, the emerging images of darker skin and afros allowed women to understand that beauty did not have to have limits. Within the mainstream black media, this change did not occur until the later 1960s and early 1970s, but its adaptation to the Black is Beautiful movement was significant for the African American community. What was once considered "militant" or "radical" became mainstream. Black Power activists worked strenuously and continuously to express the racial pride that was shadowed by white society throughout the 1960s, and finally saw results as the United States entered a new decade.

It was only a matter a time before popular black magazines and newspapers represented diversity within the black community. The rise of the Black Power era sparked a long journey that the African American community endured in order to achieve acceptance in mainstream society. Not only were they "accepted," but they created their own definitions of beauty that pervaded the minds of a variety of backgrounds. *Beautiful* was no longer synonymous with *white*. The efforts of Black Power activists and groups like AJASS shifted this narrow definition of beauty and liberated the black women who could not fit this impossible standard.

The beginning of this essay shined light on Patrice Gaines-Carter's daughter's inability to understand her mother's struggle with her own blackness that she faced during her childhood. In kindergarten, Carter was troubled by the pinkish color labeled "flesh" in her crayon box. Although pressured to use the crayon, she was defiant. She "colored [her] people purple, green, and even black."[43] When she grew up, she was aware that in order "to make sure you weren't one of the 'black' ones, there were bleaching creams, with labels like Altra and Nadinola, that promised to lighten the color of your dark skin."[44] However, her defiance from her childhood carried over to adulthood, and she never gave into that pressure to fit the white ideal. Because of women like Patrice Gaines-Carter, the Black is Beautiful movement gained momentum and followers, which eventually reshaped beauty standards for black women. Since Gaines's daughter was born after the implantation of integration and the first few murmurs of "black is beautiful," she did not have to worry about bleaching her skin or straightening her hair. Thanks to the perseverance of the Black Power activists, she could readily accept the notion that black, indeed, was beautiful.

Notes

1. Patrice Gaines-Carter, "Remembering Times Before Black Was Beautiful," *The Washington Post*, February 19, 1984, C1.
2. Tanisha C. Ford, *Liberated Threads: Black Women, Style, and the Global Politics of Soul* (Chapel Hill: The University of North Carolina Press, 2015); Susannah Walker, *Style and Status: Selling Beauty to African American Women, 1920–1975* (Lexington: University Press of Kentucky, 2007); Julia Kirk Blackwelder, *Styling Jim Crow: African American Beauty Training During Segregation* (College Station: Texas A&M University Press, 2003); Obiagele Lake, *Blue Veins and Kinky Hair: Naming and Color Consciousness in African America* (Santa Barbara: ABC-CLIO, 2003).
3. Walker, *Style and Status*, 171.
4. Lake, *Blue Veins and Kinky Hair*, 82.

5. Ford, *Liberated Threads*, 169.
6. Walker, *Style and Status*, 171.
7. Meeta Rani Jha, *The Global Beauty Industry: Colorism, Racism, and the National Body* (New York: Routledge, 2016), 32.
8. Margaret L. Hunter, "'If You're Light You're Alright': Light Skin Color as Social Capital for Women of Color," *Gender and Society* 16, no. 2 (April 2002): 190.
9. Hunter, "If You're Light You're Alright," 190.
10. Bleach and Glow Cream, Advertisement, *Ebony*, January 1961, 102.
11. Black and White Bleaching Cream, Advertisement, *Ebony*, January 1961, 58.
12. eXelento Hair Pomade, Advertisement, *Jet*, January 1961, 61.
13. Perma-Strate, Advertisement, *Ebony*, January 1960, 73.
14. "Display Ad 12," *Chicago Daily Defender*, July 11, 1963, 14.
15. "Display Ad 3," *Afro-American*, May 1961, 3.
16. "Display Ad 10," *Afro-American*, October 4, 1969, 18.
17. "Display Ad 10," 18.
18. "The Artist," Kwame Brathwaite Collection, https://www.kwamebrathwaite.com/about (accessed March 29, 2019).
19. Melissa Smith, "The Photos That Lifted Up the Black Is Beautiful Movement," *The New York Times*, November 27, 2018.
20. Richard Thompson Ford, "A Hairstyle Is Not a Civil Right: The City's Commission on Civil Rights Is Taking the Wrong Approach to a Real Problem," *New York Daily News*, March 17, 2019.
21. Kwame Brathwaite, *Untitled (Photo shoot at a school for one of the many modeling groups who had begun to embrace natural hairstyles in the 1960s)*, 1966, Kwame Brathwaite Collection, Philip Martin Gallery, Los Angeles, CA.
22. Nadja Sayej, "Black Is Beautiful: Celebrating the Significance of Kwame Brathwaite," *The Guardian*, March 26, 2019.
23. Sayej, "Black Is Beautiful."
24. Kwame Brathwaite quoted in Charlene Hunter, "Harlem Models Stress Unity Idea: A 'Naturally' Show Called Format for African Culture," *New York Times*, June 26, 1971, 20.
25. Brathwaite quoted in Hunter, "Harlem Models Stress Unity Idea," 20.
26. Ford, *Liberated Threads*, 57.
27. Ford, *Liberated Threads*, 57.
28. Kwame Brathwaite, "Art, Artists, and Activism: The Black Arts Movement Revisited," *National Conference of Artists of New York*, 2006.
29. Milburn Davis, "Lack of Racial Pride Caused by Segregation," *Afro-American* (1893–1988), October 15, 1966, 5.
30. Hasan Jeffries, *Bloody Lowndes: Civil Rights and Black Power in Alabama's Black Belt* (New York: New York University Press, 2010), 187.
31. Marcus H. Boulware, "Yes, We All Talk," *New Journal and Guide*, May 24, 1969, 7.
32. Byrne, "Expert Views on Black Beauty," H1.
33. Sandra Haggerty, "Black Is Beautiful – a Vital Concept," *Los Angeles Times*, February 8, 1970, F3.
34. Front Cover, *Ebony*, January 1970, 1.

35. Front Cover, *Ebony*, May 1974, 1.
36. Front Cover, *Ebony*, May 1974, 1.
37. Afro Sheen, Advertisement, *Ebony*, January 1969, 23.
38. Gold Medal, "Now Styles," Advertisement, *Ebony*, January 1974, 93.
39. Perma-Strate, Advertisement, *Ebony*, December 1969, 82.
40. Murray's Superior Hair Dressing Pomade, Advertisement, *Ebony*, January 1974, 56.
41. Posner, Advertisement, *Ebony*, March 1970, 3.
42. Walker, *Style and Status*, 194.
43. Gaines-Carter, "Remembering Times," C1.
44. Gaines-Carter, "Remembering Times," C1.

9. *Cosmopolitan* and *Playboy*: Complicated Beauty Ideals and 1960s Feminism

KAYA MCGEE

> How could any woman not be a feminist? The girl I'm editing for wants to be known for herself. If that's not a feminist message, I don't know what is.
>
> – Helen Gurley Brown[1]

"Beauty is in the eye of the beholder" is a timeless and applicable saying that is especially important when it comes to women. The image of a blonde, blue-eyed, busty woman in slinky clothing with innocent yet naughty eyes pulling you in appeared as the "It-girl" in a 1965 issue of *Playboy* magazine. Almost simultaneously, a darker-haired, brown-eyed woman in new-age funky threads, with eye contact so direct you are almost intimidated by her confidence and power, took over the covers of *Cosmopolitan*. These photos, alongside many other images, were forced onto women through the media to embed ideals of female beauty into their minds. These images embodied what each magazine viewed as sexy in a 1960s woman, yet they are completely different from one another. These two magazines dominated the 1960s in terms of portraying their version of the ideal woman and how that woman should be considered a sex symbol.

The feminist movement and sexual revolution were brought to life in a unique way through the images on the covers of each of these magazines. These movements allowed women to redefine what was meant to be not only sexy but sexually free with less social restriction. They facilitated independence and progress in women's rights, specifically in terms of relationships and sex. The two magazines showcased a broadening image of what was attractive and desirable, along with a multiplicity of opinions. The diverse movement created an atmosphere for men and women to have very different ideals in what they wanted to see in women, and for the female readers of *Cosmopolitan*, in themselves, as women.

The historical discussion on feminism, the sexual revolution, and specific aspects of these distinct but related movements is full of varying opinions, much like the time period itself. With special consideration of views on the female body and beauty, the issue of the male role remains a hotly debated topic. Some scholars see male participation in women's sexual revolution as degrading and perverted, while others see it as supportive of the newly found female freedom. Other historians expand this view beyond the sexualized female body into beauty and fashion. They see the feminist movement as working to diminish the once restrictive limitations on the ideals of beauty and femininity.[2] Although the scholars discuss feminism in regard to sexuality, their opinions differ on what was conducive to the movement and what involved the advantages of sexually free women.

This chapter argues that sex played a very important role not only in the feminist movement but in the way that women looked at themselves in terms of attractiveness. While the world of sex was expanding, certain societal norms remained the same or very similar to how they once had been, including the view that women lived their lives for men. Even with feminists trying to push away from that view, in terms of sex, many Americans still viewed women as an object for men. As the covers of *Playboy* and *Cosmopolitan* demonstrate, however, there was no one definition of feminism, femininity, or beauty but rather a very complicated set of standards and expectations that encompassed multiple opinions and perspectives.

This chapter will explore the different ideals in beauty by comparing *Playboy*, a male-oriented magazine, to the more female-oriented magazine, *Cosmopolitan*, asking, What do images of *Playboy* and *Cosmopolitan* reveal about the male and female views of feminism and the sexual revolution between 1964 and 1968? To do this, I will analyze the covers of each magazine, paying particular attention to hair, body language, and clothing – three categories of importance in terms of defining femininity and sex appeal in women. Along with these sources I will include books, newspaper articles, and interviews with Helen Gurley Brown and Hugh Hefner (the editors in chief of each magazine). Although both magazines supported feminism and free sexual expression, during the period between 1964 and 1968, Playboy appeared to idealize the stagnant mold of female beauty through a male perspective, while Cosmopolitan embraced beauty through new forms of self-expression.

Feminism, the Sexual Revolution, and Female Beauty

In a time of great social change, the 1960s feminist and sexual revolutions created opportunity for increased independence in women's minds and bodies. These two movements had different objectives, but in certain circumstances they meshed together in a very complicated fashion. Although the feminist movement is mainly known for advocating for women's rights in the workplace, it also reflected changes in the household.[3] This feminist fight often crossed over to fighting for women's control over their bodies and sexuality. As for the sexual revolution, it encompassed a woman's right to pleasure and sex without the stigma that a woman who had premarital sex would be looked at as loose and having less of a chance to get a husband. This idea then transitioned into women being able to define their own beauty without the sole opinion of what a man found to be sexy.[4] In many instances the sexual revolution also connected with the counterculture. As the 1960s progressed and the multiple movements gained a stronger foothold in society, many movements became intertwined. With the counterculture and the questioning of societal norms, the sexual revolution became seen as an almost "hippie" movement because of the people who supported this new lifestyle of free love.[5] This paper merges the dynamics of female appearance and sexual expression of these two separate and complex movements into one called the feminist sexual revolution.

The feminist sexual revolution went beyond women being able to have shameless premarital sex. This movement represented women being free to control their bodies in a way they had not been able to previously because of societal standards. Prior to the 1960s, women were expected to use their virginity as a tool of respectability to eventually find a husband and have children. Although some aspects of this outdated life ideal remained during the sexual revolution, for women, female empowerment became the main objective. Women began to question and challenge the typical lifestyle of marriage and children as a means to fulfillment in life.[6] They also realized that sex could be very pleasurable for them and that they could enjoy it outside of the confines of marriage. Women explored this sexual liberation not only outside this institution but also outside the heterosexual norm. Nevertheless, many women still used their looks to attract men.[7] Even though this revolution allowed women to explore their roles in society and sex, they still craved sexual approval from men.

Along with the feminist sexual revolution came a media that judged female appearance by what they deemed as most attractive. There was no shortage of newspapers and public outlets dictating what they considered the definition of female beauty to be. In the early 1960s, many people still considered women's appearance important to finding a husband. According to journalist C. C. Cabot, in terms of fashion, average men wanted women to dress nicely but not so out there as to "overshadow your personality."[8] In his opinion, women should wear typical female clothing, like dresses, that showed off their womanly attributes, such as cleavage. Another aspect of appearance the author considered crucial to attractiveness was hairstyle. He declared that men did not desire women who wore nontraditional hairstyles, especially those that did not align with that woman's age.[9] In another article, writer Dave Galloway suggested that women should be their natural selves and worry less about the "ideal" measurements since there was much more to attracting men than just physical attributes.[10] Lastly, writer Stanley Frank wrote about the increasing popularity and acceptability of hair dye products in the female community. He claimed that hair dye did not pick up in the male population because of the supposition that men "usually seek satisfaction in their work," while women "equate an attractive appearance with security."[11] Although these articles approached female beauty standards from different perspectives, what they share in common is that they were written as men's views on women's bodies. During this time, there were still plenty of men who assumed that women only cared about their looks in order to obtain men or keep their husbands' interest, without recognizing the idea that women might want to look good for themselves. These authors used their platforms to push their personal preferences of female appearance with only a male viewpoint.

Playboy

Like the previous authors, Hugh Hefner used *Playboy* to promote his view of female beauty ideals to the general public. *Playboy* was Hefner's brainchild, the product of a seemingly normal American man who grew up in a culturally conservative household. Due to the restrictive environment he was raised in, Hefner desired sexual freedom without judgment. Prior to publishing his magazine's first issue, Hefner worked as a copywriter for *Esquire*, another male-oriented magazine. In 1953, he branched out on his own with a memorable and controversial nude photo of Marilyn Monroe. Before actually employing models to pose for the centerfolds, he bought Monroe's photo for five hundred dollars.[12] The magazine quickly took off and became known for its provocative photos that challenged traditional American ideals of sex behind closed doors.

Hefner wanted *Playboy* to help change the mindset of the American people and eliminate the shame associated with premarital sex. In a 1967 interview, Hefner said that *Playboy* emphasized sex to be "heterosexual, healthy, associating sex with beauty."[13] To further elaborate in another interview, he described the purpose of the magazine:

> What made Playboy so popular was not simply the naked ladies, there were naked ladies in other magazines, what made the magazine so popular was, even before I started writing the philosophy, there was a point of view in the magazine, it prior to that you couldn't run nude pictures without some kind of rational that they were art. I made them into, I put them into a context of a positive or what I perceived as a positive attitude on male female relationships. I suggested that sex was not the enemy, that violence was the enemy, that nice girls like sex. The centerfold itself, the girl next door centerfold, in a very simplistic way was rooted in that philosophy, that that sex is OK, it's a natural part of life.[14]

This quote suggests that not only did Hefner want to portray female sexual pleasure in a more positive light but, through his work in *Playboy*, tried to destroy the notion that only immoral women had sex. He recognized that the general public viewed the act of female sexual freedom negatively. By attempting to make the act be seen as more common and less obscene, he hoped that a woman's image would no longer be tainted. From the support he gave to women being able to be seen as the girl next door yet sexually free, he became a pioneer of the female sexual revolution.

Despite his goals and position in the feminist and sexual movement, women criticized Hefner for degrading women rather than empowering them. One such writer, Gloria Steinem, went undercover and wrote an exposé of what it was like to work as a Playboy Bunny – the waitresses who served patrons drinks and cigarettes at Hefner's Playboy Clubs. Of course, being a Bunny differed from being a cover model, but she still had an overall image to keep up with. From Steinem's perspective, the job recruitment focused on an image of being a Bunny. At one point in her article, she recalled a woman saying, "We don't like our girls to have any background, we just want you to fit the Bunny Image." This look specifically included toned legs, a large bosom, and an incredibly tiny waist. They usually dressed in high heels and high-legged leotards. To help assist with this unattainable appearance, club managers had the girls walk in high heels up and down stairs to build muscle in their legs, used plastic stuffing to boost the breast area, and corsets to cinch in undesirable belly fat.[15] Steinem's article accentuated a more misogynistic side to the company, rather than the feminist one claimed by Hefner. Another female activist, Susan Brownmiller, described Hefner as her enemy on television's *Dick Cavett Show*, claiming that "the dialogue on so many of our issues were controlled by men," including men like Hefner.[16] Thus, there was a major disconnect between Hefner and many women, especially feminists, because they did not think he respected women or their rights. Nevertheless, Hefner supported the feminist movement and sexual revolution and promoted a progressive mindset in his interviews.

These photos are the September covers of Playboy magazine from 1964 to 1968. They represent the male perspective of beauty ideals during this time. As is evident from the images, the cover women almost look identical. Playboy covers, from left, September 1964, September 1965, September 1966, September 1967, September 1968.

Although Hefner openly supported feminism, his choice in models, especially when it came to their hair, did not encompass the progress made through the movement. For much of the twentieth century, long hair was considered innately feminine, which caused tension when people began to experiment outside what was considered normal. In the 1960s especially, a time when women were venturing out and exploring different hair lengths, such as very short hair, many people objected to it. Some thought that this took away from the women's femininity and made them appear more masculine. Conversely, people viewed men growing their hair out as being less manly because of the stigma that longer hair only belonged on women. Hair became particularly important when it came to the rise of lesbianism as part of the sexual revolution. Some women explored a more gender-fluid look and cut their hair short, almost boy-like.[17] The feminist sexual revolution allowed for an exploration of hairstyles that crossed gender boundaries in a way that America had not seen before.

Despite Hefner being a major ally to the sexual revolution, he did not go far to showcase women's new revolutionary hairstyles. Instead, he displayed women with hair that fit within the parameters of socially accepted femininity. In the time from 1964 to 1968, it is obvious that blonde hair was favored in *Playboy* magazine. This not only signified what the creator, Hugh Hefner, viewed as the best hair color, in terms of female sex appeal, but it also reflected what he viewed to be the most popular with a majority of men. Almost all of the covers portrayed women with blonde hair. The 1966 cover, for example, was one of the few exceptions; its design covered the model's hair so that only a peek of brown was visible. However, it is not a dark brown or black, but a lighter brown. This signified that lighter hair, in general, was more wanted in the male population than the darker variety.

Beyond the color of the hair, the style of each woman's hair is also very similar. All appear plastic-like, as if a fan could blow in their face, but their hair would not budge. With hairspray being invented a little over a decade before, it is clear that this tool was used extensively in the model's hair. Hefner chose a prim and proper look rather than an untamed messier style because of the desirability of men as well. This indicates that although men embraced sexual expression more, they still wanted women to look put together rather than unkempt.

Throughout the five-year period, the female appearance of hair choice remained stagnant with one outlier. With only one brunette in the sea of blondes and the latest blonde, in 1968, having the longest of hair, the look stayed within the same category. Considering that blonde hair in adult women was not that common, this suggests that men favored a more artificial look in women even in a time when women were accepting themselves and their natural beauty more than they had in a long time. Although the feminist sexual revolution was full steam ahead by the later sixties, the hairstyle of a woman in the male gaze did not waiver.

Similar to hair, clothing was another category that largely differentiated what was defined at the time as feminine or masculine. The feminist sexual revolution created an environment for women to defy the norms of what society deemed appropriate when it came to clothing. Although *Playboy* supported women's sexual exploration, the magazine only reflected women oozing sensuality, sometimes with cleavage peeking through their tops. The magazine only used a certain type of sexy women, not the variety that was developing throughout the movement. The covers had women with clothing that accentuated their female attributes, like breasts and curves, rather than pushing any gender boundaries of women being less busty.

Playboy was known for its risqué, fully nude centerfold photos for the pleasure of the male readers. Shockingly, yet also unsurprisingly, the covers were much less racy. This more conservative clothing choice seemed to be strategic. While some may be surprised by the amount of clothes that appeared on these women, it is important to keep in mind that this was the cover of the magazine. The goal appeared to be to entice men to buy it without giving the best parts away. The covers were meant to be sexy enough to get the man interested with the use of a beautiful woman, but not too sexy that him seeing the cover was enough and he no longer needed to buy the magazine.

The overall theme for women's clothing on *Playboy* covers is that nothing stood out too much. A 1964 cover depicted a woman with a white lace dress. The 1965 cover brought a woman in a black low-cut top with a necklace that just about reached her bosom. The following year's did not show what the woman's clothing was because we only saw her face depicted in a picket sign. A 1967 cover showed the most color, with a young woman donning an oversized green jersey with knee-high socks to match. Lastly, in 1968, the model was wearing a neutral brown turtleneck and jacket. Even though each model wore something different from the others, there was a pattern that took place in the choosing of the outfits. From looking closely at the clothing, the magazine used a neutral color palate. Another aspect seen in some of the covers, particularly 1965 and 1967, is that the clothing color also matched with the background. Perhaps men did not want female's clothes to distract from their physical beauty. Therefore, the clothes are almost unnoticed because of the bland colors, so the woman's face and body are what are at the forefront.

The neutral color palate used for the clothing emphasized the body language of the models all the more. Although women were gaining independence, the magazine reflected a submissive woman. This could have been due to the traditional role of women accepting the passive role in a relationship being upheld even through the changing times, especially when it came to sex. In other words, men still wanted to feel like a man and in control. Because of this, the magazine portrayed women as such, due to the magazine's male demographic. Throughout the following years of the sixties, the women that posed for the cover of *Playboy* appeared sexy and alluring without being too forward. To achieve this "sex kitten" vibe, they used body language.

In 1964, the model's body was angled to the side, with her face looking over her shoulder. Her hand gently rested on her face. Her eyes looked into the camera, almost pulling the viewer in. Her lips were parted ever so slightly as if she were going to ask viewers to come over and join her. Following in 1965, the woman's body faced forward, but her eyes were cast downward. She had a flirty cheek dimple peeking through, along with a closed-mouth smile. The 1966 cover differed, as readers saw only a close-up of her face. She had a toothy smile and looked to the side. The model in 1967 stood out most from the bunch because not only was her full body shown, but she also faced the camera directly. Looking more closely, one arm crossed her body to hold the helmet and her leg jutted out to the side a little. Lastly, there was the cover of the 1968 issue in which the woman featured rested her chin on her hand while her eyes peered into the camera, with her face just a tad to the left. From first glance it seems that these are a diverse variety of poses for the magazine, but with further analysis, there were apparent patterns followed throughout the years

Very much like the other categories mentioned, body language shared a consistency in elements of their posing. Elements such as these were so important, yet a lot of the time they went unnoticed. Outside of the 1967 cover, there was not one model that faced the camera head-on and had her eyes be directed forward as well. Such direct poses would make the person seem powerful and dominant, which was not the point of the pictures. The photographs were meant to appeal to men's sexuality, not create the possibility of them consciously questioning their manhood. One might have argued that 1967 could have been an anomaly that proved that Hefner, in fact, was supporting and showcasing a powerful woman, but after further examination, it also represented submissiveness. Although parts of the model faced forward, representing confidence, other parts of her body, like her legs and arms, were relaxed. This concludes that even though the magazine overall supported the rights of women, there were still limitations to how much female power men found sexy.

Playboy stood behind the ideals of free sexuality among women, but its ideals of female beauty were not as open as its sexual views. The type of woman idealized on the covers of *Playboy* were not only unrealistic but uniform. The bright blonde-haired woman with sparkling blue eyes dominated the covers with only one brunette in the mix of a five-year period. With the feminist sexual revolution raging on and evolving throughout the years, *Playboy*'s image of a woman remained stagnant in time.

Cosmopolitan

Helen Gurley Brown transformed *Cosmopolitan* magazine from the frumpy magazine written by men for housewives to vibrant articles promoting sexual freedom and pleasure for married and single women. Brown took over the magazine in 1965 and caused a stir in society with her outwardly sex-oriented articles and pictures. This viewpoint bothered many people because of how casually she discussed sex. As mentioned in her book *Sex and the Single Girl*, "Sex, as we have said, is enjoyed by single women who participate not to please a man ... but to please themselves."[18] She shattered typical ideals of sex as only for a man's enjoyment, and not all readers approved of her progressive outlook. Brown demonstrated her version of feminist beliefs within the pages of the magazine.

Similarly, to Hefner, Brown also had people who disagreed with how she interpreted sex and feminism itself. In one interview Brown recalled a time when some feminists were appalled by her portraying women as sex objects. She rebutted by saying, "It's fabulous to be a sex object. You gotta worry when nobody wants to go to bed with you."[19] What she seemed to mean by this was that you did not have to be the most beautiful woman in the world to be sexy or get ahead in the world. It was about trying to put forward your best self that did that. Brown also claimed that some men are nervous about women becoming more sexually active as well. She thought this fear stemmed from the idea that a woman could compare men sexually to one another.[20] Even though not everyone agreed with her ideology, Brown still stood as an important feminist leader of the 1960s.

These are the covers of Cosmopolitan magazines from 1964 to 1968. They show a consistent standard of beauty of brunettes. Cosmopolitan covers, from left: August 1964, September 1965, September 1966, September 1967, September 1968.

Although some people did not approve of Brown's views of sex, she did relate to many women when it came to her use of brunette models in her magazine. Playboy and Cosmopolitan shared many differences in their covers; one of them was the color of the models' hair color and style. In the 1964–1968 issues of Cosmopolitan, the women tended to have not just brown hair but dark brown hair. The 1967 cover model also did not have the bright blonde shown in Playboy but almost a light brown with blonde highlights throughout. Another factor that differed from the male magazine was the style of the hair. Unlike Playboy's cover, which kept a similar style throughout of a heavily hair-sprayed blonde, Cosmopolitan had a variety of different styles. For example, 1965's cover model had very voluminous hair, while 1966's model had a beehive half-up, half-down style. Apart from the others, 1968's model wore an updo with tighter spiral curls, which not only made her stand out from the Playboy covers but the Cosmopolitan covers as well. The two magazines' opposing views of favorable hair signified differences in male and female ideals.

The variances regarding hair between the two popular magazines say something deeper than just men and women thinking differently about beauty. *Playboy*'s preferences remained almost the same throughout the five-year period, while *Cosmopolitan*'s had considerably more variety. This suggests that women had a more open mind about what they found to be attractive than men, whose desired look remained stagnant. This also showed that women branched out from the typical opinion of blonde being beautiful and embraced brunettes more. In turn, this demonstrates that, in reference to the sexual revolution, women went beyond being more expressive sexually but also physically when it came to the ideals of attractiveness.

Much like when it came to hair, *Cosmopolitan*'s clothing choice was much more progressive than its opposite, *Playboy*. *Cosmopolitan* made the clothing more fashion forward and did this by using different colors and textures. The 1964 model wore a funky yellow-and-white patterned top, while the following year used a simple low-cut red blouse. In 1966, the model wore another red top, accessorized with big gold earrings. The 1967 model is dressed in a plunging turquoise-green top with gold accent buttons running down and hip gold armbands. Lastly, with 1968, the women had on a feathery red top. The 1967 and 1968 backgrounds match the colors of their tops, while the rest have much lighter and whiter surroundings. While *Playboy* dressed the women so that their outfits would not stand out, *Cosmopolitan* did just the opposite.

Clothing was crucial to people, in general, because it gave leeway to express personality through what they wore. *Playboy* used neutral clothing to seemingly make the women's bodies the center of attention without letting any of their personality shine through. *Cosmopolitan* took a different route and dressed the models so that their clothes had just as much character as the ladies dressed in them. The magazine used the color red frequently, which could be due to the color being used to represent power. These differences in attire could be explained by *Playboy* only wanting the female beauty to stand out; meanwhile, *Cosmopolitan* wanted the woman to have a vibrancy in herself and outside that could compete with the bold colors.

Due to the feminist background of *Cosmopolitan*, the magazine likely chose the body language of the models to be powerful and strong, but still embody sex appeal, just like their choice in fashion. In 1964, the model is facing straight forward with direct eye contact to the camera. That year was a special case because that was the year before Helen Gurley Brown took over as the editor of *Cosmopolitan* magazine, so the sexiness represented in the other models is lacking in this cover. Nonetheless, she still represents confidence rather than a feminine frailty. The next year is the same, with strong eyes and a closed mouth. In 1966, the woman is lying on her side, looking slightly off center, but her eyes are almost glaring, and lips pursed. The 1967 cover was yet another woman with softer but still confident eyes looking deep into the camera and viewers' eyes. She had a slightly closed-mouth smile, and her arms jutted out a little from her body. Lastly, in 1968, the cover had a model whose body was facing halfway to the side but face and eyes forward, with a similar stoic look. Throughout the years, the women consistently embodied a commanding, yet still flirtatious, pose, which represented Helen Gurley Brown's version of a Cosmo woman.

Conclusion

Cosmopolitan and *Playboy* both represented sexy women, but in opposing ways through their poses. *Cosmopolitan* portrayed the models as sexy but also independent. They did this through direct eye contact and a forward-facing body. This showed that the women were not just people that stood behind men but rather stood in the forefront. *Playboy* posed women to look daintier and more submissive. The magazine achieved this version of sexiness by keeping the women facing off center and making their eyes appear full of sexual desire. The body language of the models, though similar at times, was used to give off certain depictions of what a sexy woman looked like.

Cosmopolitan and *Playboy* both used the covers of their magazines to reel in customers with the image of an erotic and beautiful woman, without her being overly sexual. Because the magazines had opposite demographics, they represented sexy in two differing manners. *Cosmopolitan* viewed women as being sexy but still strong. They were females that were not just sexy for the desire of men, but sexy because they wanted to be. *Cosmopolitan* wanted to show that a woman could be sexy by being confident and different. They obtained this image by having the women look different than the normal blonde, blue-eyed girl and allowed personality to be seen through their clothes, hair, and body language. *Playboy* viewed women as almost the exact opposite. That magazine embraced the stationary version of sexy, with a bleach-blonde-haired woman. Its opinion of women still remained as being sexy for the pleasure of men. *Playboy* displayed this version of sexy not only because of the editor's personal opinions but also the magazine's male demographic. This suggests that with the rise of feminism and the sexual revolution, the view of femininity and sexual attractiveness remained unchanging for men while the women's view evolved. This could be explained by the newfound sense of freedom of expression and thought. These magazines allowed for a deeper analysis of male and female opinion on what constituted beauty and sex appeal in a time of change in the female world.

While the sexual revolution and second-wave feminism intensified as the 1960s went on, *Cosmopolitan*'s and *Playboy*'s covers remained practically the same. Even with *Cosmopolitan* favoring female expression with colorful outfits and brunettes over blondes, it, like *Playboy*, kept a similar-looking woman on its covers from 1964 to 1968. These unchanging ideals represented in both magazines suggest that even though sexuality and beauty ideals were being challenged and diversified in certain groups within the sexual revolution, these aspects could not penetrate popular media outlets, such as magazines. The sexual revolution hippy style with long tangled hair, headbands, and psychedelic patterns were nowhere to be seen in either magazine. This proposes that maybe to break through the media wall, the movements had to break through the mainstream first. *Cosmopolitan* and *Playboy* sought to represent feminine sexuality, yet even they had limitations to what being sexy looked like during the 1960s.

In a simplistic outlook, these are just magazines with pictures of pretty women for people to look at. Now it is obvious that it was much more than that. These magazines were what people saw on an everyday basis. They had the power to influence and showcase the opinion of the masses onto others. Feminist sexual freedom was not a one-size-fits-all way of thinking. The entire point was for women to have the opportunity to decide for themselves what they thought of in terms of being sexy and sexually open. This meant that magazines and other forms of public advertisement could change how women viewed themselves. Both magazines' editors showed public support for the feminist movement and the sexual autonomy that came with it. But how they portrayed attractiveness in women differed, suggesting that beauty really is in the eye of the beholder.

Notes

1. Judith Thurman, "Helenism: The Birth of the Cosmo Girl," *The New Yorker*, May 11, 2009 (accessed April 16, 2019), https://www.newyorker.com/magazine/2009/05/11/helenism.
2. David Allyn, *Make Love, Not War: The Sexual Revolution, an Unfettered History* (Boston: Little, Brown, 2000); Linda Grant, *Sexing the Millennium: Women and the Sexual Revolution* (New York: Grove, 1994); Geoffrey Jones, "Blonde and Blue-Eyed? Globalizing Beauty, c. 1945–1980," *The Economic History Review* 61 (2008): 125–54, https://www.jstor.org/stable/40057559; Nicole R. Krassas, Joan M. Blauwkamp, and Peggy Wesselink, "Boxing Helena and Corseting Eunice: Sexual Rhetoric in *Cosmopolitan* and *Playboy* Magazines," *Sex Roles* 44 (2001): 751–71, https://kmoser2.files.wordpress.com/2013/04/boxing-helena-and-corseting-eunice-sexual-rhetoric-in-cosmopolitan-and-playboy-magazines.pdf; Jo B. Paoletti, *Sex and Unisex: Fashion, Feminism, and the Sexual Revolution* (Bloomington: Indiana University Press, 2015); James Peterson, *A Century of Sex: Playboy's History of the Sexual Revolution* (New York: Grove, 1999); Carrie Pitzulo, "The Battle in Every Man's Bed: 'Playboy' and the Fiery Feminists," *Journal of the History of Sexuality* 17 (2008): 259–89, https://www.jstor.org/stable/30114220.
3. Ellen Carol Dubois and Lynn Dumenil, *Through Women's Eyes: An American History* (Boston: Bedford/St. Martin's, 2012), 678.
4. Dubois and Dumenil, *Through Women's Eyes*, 683.
5. Dubois and Dumenil, *Through Women's Eyes*, 678.
6. Dubois and Dumenil, *Through Women's Eyes*, 676, 682.
7. Dubois and Dumenil, *Through Women's Eyes*, 683; Jane F. Gerhard, *Desiring Revolution: Second-Wave Feminism and the Rewriting of Twentieth-Century American Sexual Thought* (New York: Columbia University Press, 2001).
8. C. C. Cabot, "Appearance Counts High But Don't Over Do It!," *The Atlanta Constitution*, January 3, 1963, 19.
9. Cabot, "Appearance Counts High."
10. Dave Garroway, "I've Got the Facts On Figures," *Los Angeles Times*, June 24, 1962, 24.
11. Stanley Frank, "Brunette Today, Blonde Tomorrow," *The Saturday Evening Post*, September 9, 1961.
12. Terry Gross, "Hugh Hefner on Early 'Playboy' and Changing America's Values," Fresh Air, NPR, September 28, 2017 (accessed April 16, 2019), https://www.npr.org/2017/09/28/554194378/hugh-hefner-on-early-playboy-feminism-and-changing-americas-values.
13. Hugh Hefner, "W5 Rare: Hugh Hefner Discusses Sexuality in 1976," interviewed by Charles Templeton, W5, September 10, 1967, video, 2:07,

https://www.youtube.com/watch?v=R8-XpBnDzYk.

14. Hugh Hefner, *Episode 13: Make Love, Not War (The Sixties)*, The National Security Archive, January 10, 1999, https://nsarchive2.gwu.edu/coldwar/interviews/episode-13/hefner1.html.

15. Gloria Steinem, "A Bunny's Tale: Show's First Expose for Intelligent People," *Show: The Magazine of the Arts*, May 1963, 4 (accessed April 16, 2019), http://sites.dlib.nyu.edu/undercover/sites/dlib.nyu.edu.undercover/files/documents/uploads/editors/Show-A%20Bunny%27s%20Tale-Part%20One-May%201963.pdf.

16. Hugh Hefner, Susan Brownmiller, interviewed by Dick Cavett on *The Dick Cavett Show*, CNN, 1970, video, 0:31 and 1:05, https://www.youtube.com/watch?v=vpbg-WGlCom8.

17. Dubois and Dumenil, *Through Women's Eyes*, 683; Jo B. Paoletti, *Sex and Unisex: Fashion, Feminism, and the Sexual Revolution* (Bloomington: Indiana University Press, 2015).

18. Helen Gurley Brown, *Sex and the Single Girl: The Unmarried Woman's Guide to Men* (New York: Bernard Geis Associates, 1962), 9.

19. Helen Gurley Brown, "The Open Mind: A Cosmo Girl Part 2," interviewed by Richard D. Heffner, *The Open Mind*, December 4, 1996, video, 12:05, https://www.youtube.com/watch?v=RFzqJy1jJAE.

20. Brown, "The Open Mind."

Notes on Contributors

Seth Hendrickson is a History Major at Virginia Tech, Class of 2020. Along with his history degree, he is double minoring in Political Science and Geography. Following graduation, he plans to continue his education at Virginia Tech to obtain his master's and gain certification in social studies education so he can teach history at the high school level. Seth has a historical interest in East Asian studies, specifically the histories of Japan and China, as well as ancient history and American foreign relations following World War I. This research paper stems from his interest in United States nuclear relations during the Cold War.

Brett Kershaw is a History and Political Science Major at Virginia Tech, Class of 2020. This project originated from his interest in examining the development of modern American political ideas. In the future, he hopes to pursue graduate studies in political anthropology and to advocate for the importance of freedom of expression and thought.

Claire Ko is a History Major at Virginia Tech, Class of 2019. This project grew out of her interest in women and gender studies and particularly ideas around intersectionality and race-based issues. Much of her undergraduate research focuses heavily on African American women's efforts throughout American history, specifically the civil rights movement. Following graduation, she plans to obtain her master's in Secondary Education so that she can teach history to high schoolers.

Kaya McGee is a History Major at Virginia Tech, Class of 2019. This project originated from her interest in the evolution of feminism and female sexuality in American society. Following graduation, she plans to take a year to work and gain life experiences before furthering her education at law school. With this, she hopes to assist people on issues of property rights.

Kayla Mizelle is a History Major at Virginia Tech, Class of 2019. This project originated from her interest in the 1960s student protest movements and power struggles. Following graduation, she will teach history with Teach For America and plans to continue her education by obtaining a master's in Secondary Education.

Marian Mollin (editor) is Associate Professor of History at Virginia Tech. She teaches courses on a variety of subjects, including twentieth-century US history, women's history, and historical research methods. Her own research focuses on the history of American social movements, with a particular emphasis on the intersections between gender and activism, and between religion and politics. She is the author of *Radical Pacifism in Modern America: Egalitarianism and Protest* (Philadelphia: University of Pennsylvania Press, 2006) and coeditor of *The Religious Left in Modern America: Doorkeepers of a Radical Faith* (Palgrave Macmillan, 2018).

Frank Powell is a History Major at Virginia Tech, Class of 2020, minoring in Political Science. This project stems from his interest in the Vietnam War and the antiwar movement. Frank grew up outside of Charlottesville, Virginia, and thought that comparing the antiwar movements of both his hometown school, the University of Virginia, and the university he attends, Virginia Tech, would be interesting and fulfilling. Following graduation, he hopes to attend law school or get a master's degree in education.

Brianna Sclafani is a History, Sociology, and Criminology Major at Virginia Tech, Class of 2020. Her minor in Peace Studies and Violence Prevention has led her to become a social advocate. She is most interested in Peace Studies and examining the intersections of race and class, part of the inspiration behind this project. President Lyndon B. Johnson's War on Poverty sparked her interest in antipoverty legislation and led her to discover the Model Cities Program. Brianna hopes to attain a law degree and continue her education on these issues to effect real change.

Abigail Simko is a History Major at Virginia Tech, Class of 2019. This project originated from her interest in John F. Kennedy, his assassination, and how it affected the American people. Following graduation, Abigail will be a part of the 2019 Teach For America Corps in eastern North Carolina, where she will continue to share her love of history with middle schoolers.

Gia Theocharidis is a History Major with a double minor in American Studies and War and Society at Virginia Tech, Class of 2019. This project originated from her fascination with how the black freedom struggle, specifically the Black Power movement, influenced the everyday lives and culture of Americans of all races. Although she enjoys studying the 1960s, she specializes in Revolutionary American history and intends to pursue her studies of the period. Gia plans to attend graduate school to obtain a master's degree and PhD in history immediately after graduation. She also intends on becoming a museum director and doing archival work.

Acknowledgments

Thank you, Dr. Marian Mollin, for your continued guidance, support, and inspiration. We are also grateful for Kathryn Walters's valuable feedback and direction. Robert Browder and Tyler Balli provided critical assistance through VT Publishing. This book would not have been possible without their help. Finally, we would like to thank our classmates who spent many late nights working on this publication; may you always remember the time we spent together.

Cover Image Credits

Front cover, clockwise from top left:

Robert Browder and Marian Mollin. *Campaign Buttons*. This photo is licensed under the Creative Commons Attribution-Share Alike 2.0 Generic license. Cropped and modified from original image © Joe Haupt. *Vintage United States Political Pinback Buttons, Most Presidential Candidates*. August 24, 2014 https://commons.wikimedia.org/wiki/File:Vintage_United_ States_Political_Pinback_Buttons,_Most_Presidential_Candidates_(15032627145).jpg This photo is licensed under the Creative Commons Attribution-Share Alike 2.0 Generic license found at: https://creativecommons.org/licenses/by-sa/2.0/deed.en.

Charles Levy. National Archives and Records Administration. *Mushroom Cloud Above Nagasaki after Atomic Bombing*. August 9, 1945. https://en.wikipedia.org/wiki/Nuclear_weapon#/media/File:Nagasakibomb.jpg. Public domain photo.

Student and Social Activities - Student Protest March. Courtesy of Historical Photograph Collection, Special Collections and University Archives, University Libraries, Virginia Polytechnic Institute and State University: https://imagebase.lib.vt.edu/image_viewer.php?q=V-TA0605170843.

Frank Wolfe. The Lyndon B. Johnson Library. *Vietnam War Protestors March at the Pentagon in Washington, D.C.* October 21, 1967. https://commons.wikimedia.org/wiki/File:Vietnam_War_ protestors_at_the_March_on_the_Pentagon.jpg. Public domain photo.

Back cover—top:

CaptJayRuffins. *With Congresswoman Shirley Chisholm at Site Youth Dialog Program, Model Cities Program*. 1970. https://commons.wikimedia.org/wiki/File:Youth_Dialog_Program1.jpg. This photo is licensed under the Creative Commons CC BY-SA 4.0 International license.

Back cover—bottom, from left to right:

Seattle Municipal Archives. *Fair Housing Protest, 1964*. May 10, 1964. https://www.flickr.com/ photos/seattlemunicipalarchives/4290618003/in/photolist-7x9xft-oNkTjP-6Evd2S-5BroCi-2e8gKWi-iMeym-d3T4a3-RZaY4j-RZaXnu-2detg3f-2d2dtT9-2aw1Xx2-fBFrKD-fBFtAv-ph3had-9XhXj-fBFt8k-fBVLo7-8HQNHm-fBVMxQ-fBVLSN-ajSejW-jomYUQ-joomnQ-jojMAn-fBFtUX-jonDAu-jojF9p-8qiJZC-fBFs7i-vEsSC-2d2dumo-Y4k9qN-SHe5h3-dCZz2q-jojKMT-jomD7J-Gz-kRPG-jomF63-DH7VQu-oZzquC-ajPwen-ajPwvM-fBVKXJ-9Ru44r-ajPw2z-jonM95-PfP1TB-FY3J3o-c1oD8U. This photo is licensed under the Creative Commons CC BY 2.0 license found at: https://creativecommons.org/licenses/by/2.0/.

Nijs, Jac. de. Anefo. National Archives of the Netherlands. *Opdracht Parool, Abbey Lincoln in concertgebouw*. July 13, 1966. https://www.nationaalarchief.nl/en/research/photo-collection/ aaf293ee-d0b4-102d-bcf8-003048976d84. Public domain photo.

Rob Mieremet. Anefo. National Archives of the Netherlands. *Albert Howard hield lezing over Black Panther beweging in USA in Mozes en Aaro, Bestanddeelnr 923-1651*. January 16, 1970. http://proxy.handle.net/10648/ab897188-d0b4-102d-bcf8-003048976d84. Public domain photo.

Made in the USA
Monee, IL
18 August 2021